**ISRAELI TANK BATTLES**

Below: M-48s race through the desert sands, towards the beleaguered Bar-Lev Line position at Matzmed. (IDF Archives);

# ISRAELI TANK BATTLES

## YOM KIPPUR TO LEBANON

### Samuel M. Katz

**ARMS AND ARMOUR PRESS**
London   New York   Sydney

To the 4,665 fallen of the Armoured Corps and the families they left behind . . .

First published in Great Britain
in 1988 by Arms and Armour Press, Artillery House,
Artillery Row, London SW1P 1RT.

Distributed in the USA by
Sterling Publishing Co. Inc.,
2 Park Avenue, New York, NY 10016.

Distributed in Australia by
Capricorn Link (Australia) Pty. Ltd., P.O. Box 665,
Lane Cove, New South Wales 2066, Australia.

British Library Cataloguing in Publication Data:
Katz, Samuel M.
Israeli tank battles.
1. Israel. *Taeva haganah le-Yisra'el. Gesot ha-shiryon* –
History   2. Israel–Arab Border Conflicts, 1949–
I. Title
956'.04   DS126.5
ISBN 0-85368-868-0

Designed and edited by DAG Publications Ltd.
Designed by David Gibbons; edited by Michael
Boxall; layout by Anthony A. Evans; maps drawn by
Richard and Hazel Watson; typeset by Typesetters
(Birmingham) Ltd., camerawork by E&M Graphics,
North Fambridge, Essex; printed and bound in Great
Britain by Richard Clay Ltd, Chichester, Sussex.

## AUTHOR'S NOTE

The determining of 'exact' numeric designations for various Israel Defence Forces units has never been an easy task. Almost forty years of war, and hostile neighbours on all sides, have made the Israelis extremely security conscious. The IDF has tried to keep exact battalion, brigade, and division designations secret until such units no longer feature in their order of battle; until the unit is no longer of major operational importance or until an official unit history has been published. Many units (from company to brigade level), in fact, exist in name only, called after the force's commander, desert animals or, in the case of many of the regional command reconnaissance units, after 'nuts'! The designations listed here have mainly been taken from IDF unit histories and official IDF sources that have been passed by the military censor and, it is to be hoped, are as accurate as possible.

The Hebrew terms and names for many units, positions, and weapons have been given in their transliterated form. Since written Hebrew script does not have a 'lower case' distinction, all Hebrew words are printed in SMALL CAPITALS.

## ACKNOWLEDGEMENTS

I should like to express my gratitude to the following people for their assistance in the preparation of this book: 'Bat-Sheva' and 'Miki Kaufman' from the IDF Archives, Yoav Efraati, and Andreas Constantinou. I should like to offer a very special word of thanks to Mr Joseph S. Bermudez, whose unselfishness and expertize were of such indispensable value. Last, but not least, to my loving wife, Sigalit, whose patience, love, and understanding helped me throughout the writing of the book and at all stages of its production.
Samuel M. Katz
March, 1987

# CONTENTS

# INTRODUCTION

The ceremony is emotionally charged and highly symbolic. The soldiers who have completed their three months of basic training disembark from their military transports and begin the ascent to the old Herodian fortress at Metzada overlooking the Dead Sea. Their distinctive black berets affording some protection from the brutal desert sun, they start the 45-minute climb up the narrow 'Roman snake path' towards Metzada's summit. Here they prepare for their TEKES HASHBA'A, the ceremony in which they are sworn in as soldiers in the Israel Defence Forces Armoured Corps. As the NCOs and officers shout their orders, the soldiers prepare the parade ground and themselves while puzzled tourists and proud parents look on.

Sitting in the reviewing stands, the 'top brass' look uncomfortable in their neatly pressed uniforms. As they wait for the ceremony to begin, they reflect upon their own careers, their own swearing in, and the countless battles they have since fought. Contemplating the assembled 18-year-olds, cradling their GALIL assault rifles, they think of future battles in which these young men may have to fight and die.

Dusk, and the military band plays nostalgic martial songs from the days of the PAL'MACH (Israel's pre-state élite strike companies) as the men, already fallen in by their Master Sergeants, stand at attention. Torches are lighted all around as the GOC, Armoured Corps makes a brief speech, praising the men assembled below, and telling them of the responsibilities and tasks which lie ahead. At a nearby table stacked with 'official issue' Israel Defence Forces bibles, two junior officers stand at the ready. As each man approaches, they recite the oath of allegiance which is excitedly repeated by the soldier who simultaneously and symbolically grasps his weapon and holy book of scriptures. The sworn in soldier showers the officers with a 'rare' IDF salute, is briskly handed a bible and returns to the ranks. After all have completed this ceremony, a wooden sign with the carved words 'Metzada shall not fall a second time' is set alight while the crowds of military dignitaries, soldiers and proud family members look on in silence.

This is the story of the IDF Armoured Corps in two wars: the 1973 Yom Kippur War, and the 1982 Lebanon War. It is also the story of the heroism and self-sacrifice so characteristic of the tank soldiers in both these conflicts. The Yom Kippur War was basically a tank war fought under the most arduous conditions. It was also one of modern Israel's most bitter struggles for survival. Surprised, on Judaism's holiest day, by a vicious and simultaneous surge on two fronts, it was the greatly outnumbered armoured brigades on the Golan Heights and in the Sinai Desert that stopped the Syrian and Egyptian onslaughts in some of the greatest tank battles in modern military history. In June 1982, when Israeli forces attempted to eliminate the Palestinian terrorist infrastructure from Lebanon, it was once again the armoured forces which bore the brunt of the fighting. Not only were these tank units involved in ferocious urban combat against Palestinian and leftist Muslim guerrillas in the refugee camps and squalid city slums, but they had to contend with a determined Syrian military presence in Lebanon's Beka'a Valley and in and around Beirut. During this bitter close-quarter fighting, anti-tank helicopters were introduced with devastating effects. The Armoured Corps lost many of its best soldiers in these two wars. In both conflicts that skill, dedication and heroism, which has come to personify the IDF tank soldier, was demonstrated by all ranks, from private soldier to General.

It is no coincidence that the Armoured Corps swearing in ceremony takes place at Metzada. Two thousand years earlier a small band of Jewish zealots held out against vastly superior Roman forces for two years, in the end committing mass suicide rather than submit to enslavement. The entire Jewish experience of persecution, survival, and the yearning towards the future is symbolically represented in the dusty remnants of King Herod's fortress. Metzada has evolved into an Israeli version of the Rock of Gibraltar. The tank skeletons lying undisturbed in the 'Valley of Tears', 'Chinese Farm', El Baas and Sultan Yakoub are memorials and testaments to the brave fighters of HEYL SHIRION who through courage have assured that 'Metzada will not fall a second time'.

**Below:** MAG'ACHIM from 14th Armoured Brigade deploy for battle during the battle of 14 October. These vehicles are changing firing positions to confuse enemy artillery spotters. (IDF Archives)

# 1973
# THE YOM KIPPUR WAR ON THE GOLAN HEIGHTS

## THE AUTUMN EARTHQUAKE — WAR ON THE GOLAN HEIGHTS

On 13 September 1973, a patrol of IAF (Israel Air Force) F-4Es, RF-4Es and Mirage IIICs (on an ambush mission themselves) were ambushed by Syrian MiG-21s while flying a reconnaissance mission near the Syrian Mediterranean port of Latakia. In the dogfight which followed, thirteen Syrian warplanes were downed, with no Israeli losses. Expecting Syrian retaliation, IDF Northern Command put its Golan Heights forces on alert. ROSH HA'SHANA leave for many of the troops was cancelled, and combat engineers worked feverishly around the clock, building two new bridges across the River Jordan, while anti-tank ditches and defensive earth ramparts were improved and strengthened.

Israel had captured the 480 square miles of the Golan Heights on the last two days of the 1967 Six Day War. The capture of the 'Heights', a plateau perched above Israeli northern settlements and dotted with numerous TELs (volcanic cones), had been a decisive and strategic victory for Israel. Population centres were no longer the targets of Syrian artillery harassment, and the crucial headwaters

of the River Jordan were in Israeli hands. Israel also gained an invaluable observation and electronics Intelligence-gathering post on Mount Hermon (JEBEL E-SHEIKH), fondly known as the 'eyes of Israel'. It was no secret that the Syrians wished to regain the heights, but A'MAN (Hebrew acronym for IDF Military Intelligence) was sure that the Syrians knew better than to tangle with the mighty IAF. This posture of confidence had been reinforced a year earlier in a series of tank skirmishes back and forth over the 'Purple Line' (the 1967 ceasefire line separating the two nations), where Syrian armour faired poorly. When Syrian forces began their impressive buildup along the Purple Line (as did Egyptian forces along the Suez Canal), only a few senior IDF officers expected war, but when these forces began to increase in size each day, IDF front-line commanders began implementing contingency plans for the inevitable show-down.

The Syrian battle plan called for the capture of the entire Golan and to reach the River Jordan by the end of the first day's fighting. They knew that in order to achieve this objective they would have to field a large and powerful force, to defeat the IDF's qualitative edge. By 2 October 1973, the Syrians had amassed across the Purple Line three infantry divisions (5th, 7th (including a Moroccan infantry brigade) and 9th) with mechanized elements, ten commando battalions, and two armoured divisions (1st and 3rd). This force totalled 1,500 tanks (T-62s, and T-55/54s with forty PT-76 amphibious tanks, eighteen World War Two vintage SU-100s, and even a few German PZKW IVs) – 900 on the front lines, 500 in the Katna-Kaswe area, and 100 belonging to the Republican Guard (whose main military task is the protection of the regime in Damascus, and is under the command of Rifa'at Assad, brother of President Assad) in

**Right:** Tank officers parade for inspection after completing officer's course, May 1973. Five months later these men would find themselves in the forefront of some of the fiercest tank battles in military history. (IDF Archives)

the Damascus area. On the front line as well, the Syrians fielded 155 artillery and heavy mortar batteries, dozens of surface-to-air missile batteries, including SAM-2, SAM-3, SAM-6s, as well as radar-controlled mobile anti-aircraft guns, such as the lethal ZSU-23-4. The Syrians had developed a lethal 'missile umbrella' all the way to Damascus, protecting their forces from the IAF.

The Israelis had noticed that the Syrians had abandoned their second lines of defence, and that the men of the two armoured divisions stationed in Katna and Kiswe, had been placed in emergency positions. IDF Northern Command could draw but one conclusion – the Syrians intended to attack!

Northern Command GOC, Major-General Yitzhak 'Hacka' Hofi, ordered mobilization plans to be reviewed and perfected. Facing the Syrians across the Purple Line, the smaller Israeli force consisted of one regular division, commanded by Brigadier-General Rafael 'Raful' Eitan (called UGDAT RAFUL, or 'Division Raful'), consisting of two battalions of infantry, eleven artillery batteries, and its main strength: the BARAK Brigade equipped with SHO'T (Centurion MBT) tanks. The 188th or BARAK (Hebrew for lightning) Brigade was spread out along the entire front line of the Golan and, in the event of war, was responsible for defending all points south of Nafekh to the Jordanian frontier. The BARAK Brigade was IDF Northern Command's 'regular' armour brigade. Formed in 1969, the brigade was responsible for 'security' duties on the Golan and the Lebanese frontier. It participated in the numerous fire-fight duels across the Purple Line in the years prior to the 1973 War, and distinguished itself in operations against PLO positions in Lebanon's Fatahland. The brigade's commander was Colonel Yitzhak Ben-Shoham who, following a stint as an instructor at the IDF's Staff and Command College, received command of BARAK in mid-1973. Born in Turkey, Ben-Shoham was an inspiring leader, who began his military career as an officer in the GIVA'ATI Infantry Brigade, eventually switching to tanks, where he was described as a 'natural' among armour officers.

Originally, the OZ, or 77th Battalion of the élite 7th Brigade, was brought up to the Golan as the BARAK Brigade's reinforcement in response to the developing military situation. The 77th Battalion was regarded as the finest

tank unit in the IDF, and its commander, Lieutenant-Colonel Avigdor Kahalani, had received the OT HAMOFET (Exemplary Service Medal) as a 7th Brigade company commander in Sinai during the 1967 Six Day War. Eventually the entire 7th Brigade was mobilized for service in the Golan. The 7th Brigade was commanded by Colonel Avigdor 'Yanush' Ben-Gal. A career armour officer, Yanush had risen through the ranks of the 7th Brigade, although he had to be 'forced' by superior officers to attend the officer's course. Yanush's disdain for military pomp, ceremony and discipline gave him a reputation for being a 'soldier's officer'. His men obeyed his orders fervently, and he was known never to question the decisions or judgement of his field officers. He was regarded as a decisive commander with brilliant tactical intuition and compelling leadership qualities.

The principal objective for Israeli forces on the Golan in the event of war was to contain enemy offensive capabilities (with the assistance of massive air support) in time for reservist brigades to mobilize and join battle. After decisively defeating enemy formations, the full-strengthed Israeli forces would go on the offensive. Behind the Purple Line lay a series of seventeen MUTZAVIM (fortifications). These position were fortified by mines and barbed wire, and lay behind anti-tank obstacles (with the exception of MUTZAV 107 which was between the Purple Line and the anti-tank defences and which amazingly was cut off throughout the Syrian blitz, but was regularly resupplied by tank platoons). Each position was manned by approximately fifteen infantrymen (mainly soldiers from the GOLANI Brigade, with some artillery and Intelligence personnel) and was supported by armoured platoons. The MUTZAVIM were intended to deal with major outbreaks of artillery and tank fire, and act as obstacles in the way of an enemy attack. The armoured clashes of the winter of 1972–3 led IDF Northern Command to improve, lengthen and flood the 5-metre deep anti-tank ditch along the Purple Line. Designed primarily to slow down a Syrian armour advance, the ditch was to channel oncoming armoured formations into predetermined 'killing grounds'. Covering these were 2.5-metre high elevated earth ramps (specifically designed for the Centurion's −9° gun depression), from which tanks, in hull-down positions, could bring accurate fire to bear on armour below.

The Syrians had also learned valuable lessons from the winter fighting of 1972–3. A series of highly concentrated anti-tank defences were set up between the Purple Line and Damascus; similar to, though stronger and more elaborate in nature than the Israeli MUTZAVIM. A large-scale exercise was held (in fact, an exact replica of their attack on 6 October 1973) in which the bridging of anti-tank obstacles was perfected. Infantry and commando formations equipped with RPG-7 and SAGGER anti-tank missiles were trained as 'mobile' tank killer teams to take advantage of the Israeli use of armour without organic infantry support.

On Friday, 5 October, the eve of Yom Kippur, the holiest of all days in Judaism, when man and creator settle all accounts, the highest state of alert, Alert GIMEL (C), was declared by IDF GHQ for the standing army. The advance headquarters of Northern Command was moved up to the Golan, and reserve units were ordered to be ready for mobilization at a moment's notice. The MUTZAVIM were reinforced, the 7th Brigade concentrated around the headquarters of UGDAT RAFUL at Nafekh, and last-minute minelaying and batalion-level reconnaissance patrols were initiated. Artillery commanders were ordered to prepare targets and firing tables, and be ready for immediate action. Following a briefing by the brigade Intelligence officers, Colonel Ben-Shoham and the commanding officers of BARAK Brigade met in an all-night session, discussing the pressing military situation, while Yanush accompanied his officers on a terrain familiarization 'outing' to study the topography around the front line. Throughout 5 October, the roads leading up to the Golan were blocked by enormous traffic congestion, as men and matériel were rushed to the centres of mobilization. Northern Command was fighting a losing battle against time.

## THE ATTACK

All was quiet in the early morning of 6 October even as brigade commanders were called to an urgent meeting at Major-General Hofi's headquarters to be told of the imminence of attack. Although all front-line units were in their highest state of alert, it was Yom Kippur, and most soldiers were praying inside the confines of their bunkers, tank refuelling depots, and machine-gun nests of the MUTZAVIM. Many of the troops were fasting, deep in prayer, and could be seen walking their posts in full combat gear, complemented with prayer shawl, and SIDUR (prayer-book). Inside the Mount Hermon complex, services were held behind the already locked steel doors. Major-General Hofi had informed his brigade commanders that the Syrian attack was expected to begin at 18.00 hours.

At 13.45 hours, artillery spotters on Mount Hermon noticed that the Syrians were removing the camouflage nets from artillery pieces stationed just across the Purple Line. Moments later, as these reports were conveyed to the forward headquarters of UGDAT RAFUL, the first of thousands of shells rained down on Israeli positions along the entire length of the front. The aerial and artillery onslaught lasted

**Right:** A Centurion belonging to an unidentified battalion within the 7th Armoured Brigade races towards the front line hours after the Syrian assault on 6 October 1973. (IDF Archives)

fifty minutes, and caused confusion among the Israelis, although damage to the positions, men and matériel was minimal. At 14.45 hours, heliborne units of the Syrian 82nd Paratroop Battalion began to land on Mount Hermon. Three Syrian Mi-8 helicopters landed their commandos (a fourth was hit by .50 machine-gun fire, exploding in mid-air), one mile from the peak, and they raced up the slopes towards the Israeli positions. Considering the vital importance of Mount Hermon, it was poorly defended by just thirteen combat soldiers from the GOLANI Brigade, led by only one officer. The numerous other non-combatant support and Intelligence personnel stationed there were inadequate, technically and psychologically, to cope with such a determined and capable attacking force. Although the outnumbered defenders put up a stiff resistance, the position fell a few hours later, with Soviet advisers being the first to 'observe' the captured electronics equipment. The fall of Mount Hermon was a

major setback for Israel; the Syrians had achieved in the opening hours of battle an important tangible as well as psychological victory.

The impressive 50-minute air and artillery barrage shocked the Israeli forces (the Syrian blitz coincided with an Egyptian attack of even greater magnitude along the Suez Canal). In skies once uncontested the Syrian Air Force mounted strafing and bombing runs against IDF positions throughout the Golan (a staff meeting at Raful's headquarters at Nafekh was 'interrupted' by MiG-19s). Immediately following the barrage, Syrian armour and infantry formations in huge waves streamed across the Purple Line. Tanks from the 7th Brigade were already engaging and destroying Syrian targets from their ramps, yet the waves of armour and mechanized infantry continued to swarm toward the MUTZAVIM. The main thrust was reported to be in the Kuneitra opening between MUTZAV 105 and MUTZAV 107, just

south of Jubat-el-Hashab. An additional attack was mounted along the Tapline Route, in the area of MUTZAV 117. These positions, held by the 7th Brigade, were attacked by the Syrian 7th Infantry Division together with elements of the 3rd Armoured Division. The first reports from both the 7th and BARAK Brigades looked promising. Their positions on the ramps were

holding the line, and a large number of Syrian tanks had been put out of action by the 'accurate' SHO'T gunners. By 17.00 hours, Major-General Hofi realized the strength of the Syrian attack, and that an extremely serious and precarious situation was developing. He ordered the entire 7th Brigade to position itself on the line, giving them responsibility for the

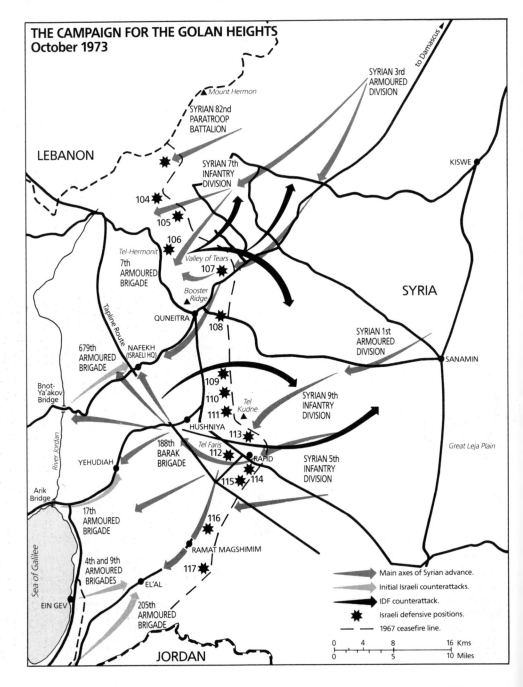

### THE CAMPAIGN FOR THE GOLAN HEIGHTS
### October 1973

to Damascus

SYRIAN 3rd ARMOURED DIVISION

Mount Hermon

SYRIAN 82nd PARATROOP BATTALION

LEBANON

SYRIAN 7th INFANTRY DIVISION

KISWE

104

105

106

Tel-Hermonit
7th ARMOURED BRIGADE

Valley of Tears
107

Booster Ridge

SYRIA

QUNEITRA

108

SYRIAN 1st ARMOURED DIVISION

SANAMIN

679th ARMOURED BRIGADE

NAFEKH (ISRAELI HQ)

Tapline Route

Bnot-Ya'akov Bridge

109

110

Tel Kudne

111

SYRIAN 9th INFANTRY DIVISION

Great Leja Plain

River Jordan

HUSHNIYA

113

188th BARAK BRIGADE

Tel Faris
112

RAFID

115    114

SYRIAN 5th INFANTRY DIVISION

YEHUDIAH

Arik Bridge

17th ARMOURED BRIGADE

116

RAMAT MAGSHIMIM

Sea of Galilee

4th and 9th ARMOURED BRIGADES

117

EL'AL

EIN GEV

205th ARMOURED BRIGADE

Main axes of Syrian advance.

Initial Israeli counterattacks.

IDF counterattack.

Israeli defensive positions.

1967 ceasefire line.

0    4    8    16 Kms
0    5    10 Miles

JORDAN

entire northern Golan, from MUTZAV 110 to Tel-Hazeika; all positions south were delegated to the BARAK Brigade. By nightfall, the severity of the military situation became obvious. The 7th Brigade was facing a major night attack by a well-organized and equipped division-size force, while the BARAK Brigade was forced to hold the Hushniyah area with only 58 tanks against the Syrian's 600.

## THE BLIGHT OF THE BARAK BRIGADE

At 14.21 hours a major Syrian advance was reported in progress towards MUTZAV 111. This force of thirty tanks, led by MTU-55 bridgelayers, and supported by mechanized infantry, moved steadily across the Purple Line. Although the small defensive force from the BARAK Brigade destroyed large numbers of enemy tanks and vehicles, it was unable to hold the line. Colonel Ben Shoham was forced to further deplete his reserve strength by sending his 2nd Battalion into battle. No matter how

many Syrian tanks were hit by the hard-pressed Israeli forces, twice that many would follow behind, continuing their advance. Assessing the Israeli situation as hopeless, the commander of the Syrian 9th Division decided to mount an additional combined armour and infantry effort to achieve a major breakthrough. Meanwhile, Ben-Shoham left the BARAK Brigade's forward headquarters at Nafekh, and set out for Al-Jukhadar along the Tapline Route, in order to consolidate the shattered remnants of his brigade. One company, commanded by Major Dani Levin, was hurriedly sent into the area just south of El-Al to stem a reported Syrian breakthrough, while Ben-Shoham kept one company for himself. Five kilometres from Al-Jukhadar, Ben-Shoham's force was ambushed by Syrian commandos. Firing Drugenov 7.62mm sniper rifles at the Israeli tank commanders, the commandos proceeded to destroy the immobilized tank with RPG fire. The fire-fight lasted two hours, with the tankers forced to use their small arms and their turret-mounted .50 machine-guns in a 360° radius. In the end, the commando force was wiped out, but it had managed to destroy four of Ben-Shoham's tanks.

**Below:** The race against time, 6 October 1973, 12.00 hours. The roads leading to the Golan Heights were jammed with men and matériel attempting to reach the front before the expected Syrian attack. (The Hebrew sign on the bumper reads: 'Warning-Irregular Cargo'). (IDF Archives)

Three kilometres from Al-Jukhadar, Ben-Shoham's already battered force came under an intense Syrian artillery barrage. Every attempt to reach Major Oded Erez's 53rd Battalion met with a barrage as the Syrians were monitoring Ben-Shoham's communications network. Major Erez notified Ben-Shoham of the desperate shortage of ammunition his unit faced, and it was decided that the ammunition supply convoy would rendezvous with his forces on the Tapline. Suddenly, and out of nowhere, a lone tank appeared, moving slowly along the Tapline. Assuming it was a damaged Israeli tank returning to Nafekh, no particular attention was paid to this now familiar sight. But when Major Erez informed Ben-Shoham that none of his tanks had left the area, a now concerned Ben-Shoham sent his operations officer, Captain Giora, to identify the lone vehicle. The tank was now ten metres from Ben-Shoham's command halftrack, when Captain Giora ran towards it, 'ordering' the tank commander to

**Right:** A platoon commander's tank (marking on mudguards reads '1st platoon commander') heads towards the battle for Tel-Hazeika. (IDF Archives)

**Far Right:** A Centurion crew from the 74th Battalion sit nervously beside their .03 calibre machine-gun awaiting the Syrian onslaught. When the Syrians actually did attack at 14.00 hours, this crew and hundreds like it sprang into action, racing towards the pre-designated firing positions along the Purple Line. (IDF Archives)

return to the front line. The tank crew panicked, slammed their flaps shut, and left the area at full speed. Captain Giora returned to Ben-Shoham's vehicle with a shocked expression, shouting, 'a Syrian tank', a Syrian tank!' This was too close a call for a brigade command group and ammunition convoy without adequate protection, so it was decided to return to Nafekh, to organize a new and more powerful force strong enough to counter-attack. The situation along the front was becoming more desperate. The Kudne line had disintegrated and Syrian armour was reported on the Tapline near Hushniya. A sizeable Syrian force had broken through near El-Al, and MUTZAVIM 115 and 116 were overrun (although the force inside these positions refused to surrender, and continued the battle). The Syrians had more than 140 tanks in the Kudne area, 60 on the Tapline, 80 attacking MUTZAV 116, and 60 attacking MUTZAV 115. The BARAK Brigade could field only fifteen tanks.

**Right:** The charred remains of a Syrian T-55 near MUTZAV 110. The Golan's flat plateau, clearly seen in the background of this photograph, proved to be ideal for armoured warfare. (IDF Archives)

## KOACH TZVIKA AND REPRIEVE

At this time, something just short of a miracle was under way at Nafekh. Frantically trying to reach the Golan by any means possible was Captain Tzvi 'Tzvika' Greengold who had been on a fortnight's leave. He arrived at Nafekh searching for a force to command. Four damaged tanks arrived at Nafekh, and the BARAK Brigade's second in command, Colonel Yisraeli, ordered Greengold to take them, and to be known on the brigade communications network as KOACH TZVIKA (Force Tzvika). Tzvika assisted his men to remove the dead and wounded from the recently arrived vehicles and raced towards the Tapline Route. Along the way, KOACH TZVIKA came into contact with a company of Syrian tanks. Tzvika reported the situation to Ben-Shoham and entered the

battle. It was now 21.00 hours on 6 October.

On hearing that KOACH TZVIKA was being fired on along the Tapline, Ben-Shoham realized his force was completely surrounded, and that it would be impossible to return to Nafekh as had been scheduled. Instead, he headed west, towards the settlement of Ramat Magshimim, where he positioned his halftrack and few tanks along the Gamla Rise, on the Ein Gev road, close enough to see the Sea of Galilee and the Israeli heartland. From here Ben-Shoham attempted to reorganize the remnants of the BARAK Brigade. Major Erez's 53rd Battalion, reduced to only six tanks, was defending the area between the Tapline and MUTZAV 115, while a company of tanks which had run out of ammunition attempted to hold off the Syrian advance towards Kuneitra, between MUTZAV 111 and Hushniya. Cut off from his men, tired, and overwhelmed by the event of the past twelve hours, Ben-Shoham spoke to his men in a calm, soothing manner, urging them to hold on and promising that the reservists would soon be on their way. But the BARAK Brigade's actual status was only too clear to those remaining along the line.

At 03.44 hours, Tzvika reported in to Ben-Shoham. He said that he was fighting along the Tapline Route, and that all 'looked well'; although Ben-Shoham could determine from Tzvika's apprehensive voice that most of his accompanying tanks had been lost. The entire brigade knew of KOACH TZVIKA, and the existence of a 'force' had sharply increased the morale of the BARAK fighters. Little did they realize that this *ad hoc* 'task force', now consisted of one incredible Captain fighting alone against the Syrian attempts to breakthrough, and at odds of 50:1. Tzvika also realized that he was alone, and decided to fight in his own way. Rather than advance along the Tapline Route as ordered, he placed his tank in a hull-down position, and waited for the enemy. Tzvika's one-man war against the Syrians became an epic. He waited for the Syrians to approach to within twenty yards of his position, then opened fire. He destroyed the first tank at such close range that the concussion put his communications set out of order. He then leaped out of the tank, changed places with the commander of another tank, and hand-signalled to the two remaining tanks to imitate his every move. After knocking out three tanks in rapid succession, he discovered that his accompanying tank was in flames. Tzvika was on his own; and heading directly for his position was a column of thirty Syrian tanks, together with supply trucks travelling in 'parade formation'. Tzvika allowed the Syrians to get close, continually firing and changing his position. This game of hide-and-seek convinced the Syrians that they were facing a much larger Israeli force. After losing ten tanks and eight trucks, the Syrian withdrew.

At this juncture the first IDF reservist units arrived at the scene, and KOACH TZVIKA was joined by, and incorporated into, the reserve 17th Armoured Brigade. Its commander, Colonel Ran Sarig received the order from Ben-Shoham to mount a counter-attack, and proceeded southwards along the Tapline Route, while Tzvika and a platoon of tanks drove parallel along the route's wire fences. After holding the Syrians for three hours, the 17th Armoured Brigade was wiped out. Lieutenant-Colonel Uzi Mur (the brigade's deputy commander) was blown out of his command tank, and critically wounded. Tzvika, sensing disaster, had pulled his forces back, and decided to wait for the Syrians near the Tapline Route's fence. But seconds later, all three of Tzvika's tanks were in flames. Tzvika leaped out of his tank, and smothered his flaming coveralls in the dust. Not realizing the extent of his wounds, he ran towards another tank, shouted garbled instructions, took command of the vehicle, and activated the communications system announcing to all the existence of 'KOACH TZVIKA'.

Ben-Shoham, who had waited until daylight to attempt to rejoin his brigade, asked General Hofi for authorization to command all forces in the southern Golan. It was clear to both men that the Syrians were swarming all over the southern part of the heights, and that most of the Israeli forces were cut off, leaderless, and disorganized. Permission was granted to Ben-Shoham.

Two kilometres from Al-Jukhadar, Major Erez's request for air-support at first light was granted; four A-4 Skyhawks flew in combat formation towards the Syrian forces assembled below. As the men of 53rd Battalion joyously cheered at the sight of the Star of David markings on an aircraft, the four planes exploded in mid-air. A second flight of Skyhawks appeared, and two more exploded above the now horrified soldiers. Major Erez requested no more air strikes that day. Ben-Shoham ordered that the 53rd Battalion regroup, but a Syrian breakthrough north of the Tapline Route had cut off the remainder of his troops from the command post. Major Erez received permission from Ben-Shoham to withdraw, and the remnants of the BARAK Brigade, twelve tanks in all, headed towards Tel Faris.

Throughout the night of 6/7 October, the Syrians had achieved major military successes in the southern part of the Golan. The 47th Tank Brigade of the 5th Infantry Division achieved a major breakthrough in the Rafid area, while the 132nd Mechanized Brigade fanned out along the Rafid El-Al road, and at dawn's first light on 7 October, the 132nd linked up at Ramat Magshimim. Victory was being prematurely celebrated in the Syrian camp, as Syrian forces were able to gaze upon the Sea of Galilee, Tiberius, and central Israel. Realizing the stiff resistance they were facing in the north, the Syrians decided to take advantage of the crumbling Israeli position in the south. With a force of more than 600 tanks, the 1st and 3rd Armoured Divisions were directed through the Rafid opening in a major push to defeat the Israelis decisively. All that stood in their way were the 'surviving' six tanks of Major Oded Erez's 53rd Battalion and the first trickle of reservists making their way to the front.

MUTZAV 117 (itself surrounded and under intense pressure) reported a large Syrian force breaking through northwards along the Tapline. From his forward position, Ben-Shoham

**Right:** War! A squad of Centurions supported by a platoon command M3 halftrack engaged Syrian armour attempting to breach the Purple Line defences near Rafid. Note aerial recognition markings on halftrack. (IGPO)

identified the advancing Syrian columns, and opted to regroup his forces at Nafekh rather than make a suicidal stand. His tank and half-track raced up the Gamla Rise towards Nafekh, dodging cannon and RPG fire along the entire route. Ben-Shoham, who by now realized that his brigade had been all but destroyed except for a few surviving platoons fighting for their lives along the Tapline Route, decided to join his deputy, Colonel Yisraeli, Tzvika, and the reservists from Colonel Uri Orr's 679th Reserve Armoured Brigade (now reaching the front in small numbers). Every three tanks now reaching the front were assembled into makeshift platoons, patched into the communications network and rushed towards Ben-Shoham's position. All in all, two companies were pieced together, and the newly formed units reached Nafekh and re-established the BARAK Brigade's headquarters. At Nafekh, the sight of this new force made UGDAH commander Raful a very relieved man. Although the military situation was critical on the

southern Golan, the Israelis were slowing down the Syrian advance, and reservists were reaching the front.

At 11.45 hours, a lead element from the Syrian 1st Armoured Division, a force of 83 tanks, attacked the six remaining tanks from the 2nd Battalion parallel to the Tapline near Hushniya. Ben-Shoham urged the young captain commanding the 2nd Battalion – wounded and out of ammunition – to hold at any cost, but the Syrian force was too strong, and he was not heard from again. Fears as to the fate of the 2nd Battalion were substantiated when Syrian tanks were seen in the area of Tel Abu Hanzir. Outflanked, Nafekh was now threatened. Raful ordered Ben-Shoham to return to Nafekh for the base's defence, and ordered deputy brigade commander Lieutenant-Colonel Yisraeli personally to set out and cover his force. Ben-Shoham's tank came under heavy Syrian artillery and tank fire throughout his retreat. Both he and Yisraeli succeeded in destroying more than twenty Syrian tanks and vehicles. As the

battle raged and Syrian tanks approached to close range, Yisraeli learned from his gunner that the tank was out of ammunition. Yisraeli ordered his driver to charge an oncoming T-62 with machine-guns blazing. Within moments, his tank in flames, Lieutenant-Colonel Yisraeli was dead. Ben-Shoham, unaware of the fate of his deputy, continued to issue orders. Standing upright in the turret, Ben-Shoham and the BARAK Brigade operations officer, Major Benny Katzin, observed the battle, firing at Syrian crewmen fleeing their burning vehicles. Searching the hills for Syrian commandos, their tank

passed a smoking T-62, when a sudden 7.62mm volley was fired from just below the tank. Ben-Shoham and Major Katzin were killed and the BARAK Brigade was now leaderless!

As the Syrians continued their push, Nafekh prepared for battle. Lieutenant-Colonel P., a senior officer on Raful's staff, organized Nafekh's defences and issued anti-tank weapons to the soldiers manning the outer perimeter. Standing at the southern perimeter fence, he watched Syrian tanks advance to a range of 2,000 yards and closing. Raful surveyed the

**Right:** A dead Syrian tanker lies next to a destroyed T-55 at the gates of Nafekh, 7 October 1973. (IDF Archives)

**Right:** A Centurion hit during the initial Syrian assault near MUTZAV 107 on 6 October. (IDF Archives)

oncoming Syrian armour dispassionately and ordered his advanced headquarters group to withdraw from Nafekh. As his halftrack left the base, hundreds of Syrian shells rained down on the camp. Syrian tanks were now entering Nafekh unhindered, firing point-blank at the base's evacuated buildings. The scene was sheer panic as coaxial and turret-mounted 14.5mm machine-guns raked the scurrying Israeli defenders. Lieutenant-Colonel P. grabbed the division's deputy Intelligence and operations officers, a bazooka and six shells, and rushed to try and stop the Syrians from taking Nafekh. Suddenly, the 679th Reserve Armoured Brigade arrived to save the day. Firing at long range, the 679th managed to hold the Syrians and push them out of Nafekh. Yet Syrian tanks were still inside the base, and Lieutenant-Colonel P.'s determined anti-tank unit was cornered by a T-62. The team fired, and missed. It was their last round. As the T-62's turret swivelled towards them, it went up in a flaming ball. Approaching the rescued officers was a battered tank moving at slow speed. It was KOACH TZVIKA! Tzvika had escaped Ben-Shoham's fate by avoiding the Tapline Route for fear of ambush. Instead he had moved alone towards Nafekh camp, firing wildly at anything that moved. Captain Greengold had been fighting for 24 hours continuously. Tzvika, bleeding, blonde hair turned black, and Nomex

**Left:** Some of Nafekh's relieved defenders enjoy a well-deserved cigarette by the remains of a Syrian T-54 destroyed by bazooka fire. (IDF Archives)

**Below:** HESDER Orthodox seminary students serving on the Golan Heights near MUTZAV 107 take a breather under the protection of their tank's camouflage covering. Highly motivated with religious zeal and tenacity, the HESDER soldiers fought surprisingly well throughout the Golan Heights campaign. (IDF Archives)

coveralls glued to his burned body, got down from his tank and gazed at the ruins of a once thriving divisional headquarters. He then broke down in tears and said he could not continue. For his incredible 24 hours on the Golan, Captain Greengold was awarded the OT HAGVURA (Order of Bravery), the IDF's medal for supreme valour.

## SAVING THE BRIDGES AND THE FRONT

The BARAK Brigade's suicidal stand in and around Nafekh had bought just enough time for the first reservist units to reach the southern Golan. The very fact that the reservists were already making their way to the front was in

itself a remarkable feat, even by IDF standards. Usually the reserves are given ample time to mobilize, during which they are supplied, briefed, and enabled to adjust psychologically from civilian life to active service. The Yom Kippur War afforded the IDF no such luxury. The reservists were literally pulled out of synagogues, from Tel-Aviv beaches, and family gatherings; and within 24 hours found themselves fighting for the very survival of their nation. IDF studies have found that on the battlefield, the MILUIM (reservists) have outperformed their conscript counterparts, yet in 1973 reserve brigade commanders faced an enormous task in the bonding of their units into effective fighting forces. Facing such a problem was Colonel Uri Orr, commander of the 679th Reserve Armoured Brigade. Originally the brigade was on its way to Kuneitra to assist the 7th Armoured Brigade, but along the route Orr received a panic-stricken distress call

from Raful's headquarters at Nafekh, telling him that the Syrians were inside the Nafekh compound. Orr's Brigade swung round and headed for Nafekh where they linked up with KOACH TZVIKA. In a close-range battle, fought at ranges of less than 10 metres, the 679th Brigade managed to relieve the pressure on Nafekh. By nightfall, the Syrians had been pushed out of Nafekh and the surrounding areas, but the Syrian 1st Armoured Division continued its drive towards the bridge across the River Jordan. By the Bnot-ya'akov Bridge, surviving officers from the BARAK Brigade had been left, charged with the bridge's defence and demolition. The sight of Israeli soldiers with-

drawing in defeat horrified them; clearly the IDF was not at its best when withdrawing. It was clear to these officers that the men *had* to be 'whipped back to shape'. Every soldier and tank was stopped, and forged into cohesive fighting units. The defensive lines were strengthened; platoons and companies made up from the lost and confused remnants of a once mighty division. As night fell, the 'last-stand commandos' (as they would be known on UGDAT RAFUL's communications network) were ordered to 'hold until relieved!' That night the men in the line wondered just how long could they really hold on? How long would it take for the reservists to arrive in full strength?

**Below:** The Bnot-ya'akov Bridge, 4 October 1973. Days later, a few fatigued men, tanks and this bridge were all that stood between the Syrians and victory. (IDF Archives)

At daybreak on 8 October the situation looked grim for the Israelis on the southern Golan. The Syrians had captured Ramat Magshimim, and were only 900 yards from El Al. The 132nd Mechanized Brigade had even reached the old Syrian works to divert the head-waters of the River Jordan on the Gamla Rise. Lead elements of the 47th Armoured Brigade were now only six miles from the Jordan.

Northern Command reserve forces consisted of two divisions: UGDAT LANER commanded by Major-General (Res.) Dan Laner, and Major-General Moshe 'Musa' Peled's UGDAT MUSA; the latter was considered the more battle-ready, having undergone large-scale manoeuvres

months prior to outbreak of hostilities. Major-General Peled, who had been relieved of his command in order to pursue university studies, was mobilized in the early morning of 6 October. On reaching the front, Peled faced enormous difficulties in organizing his forces. Besides an impending order from GHQ to move south towards the Suez front, Peled discovered that his equipment was not only obsolete (with two of his brigades equipped only with modernized M-51 Sherman tanks), but dispersed on loan to units in training and those guarding the Israeli-Lebanese border. Peled formed a special unit of his most able officers and ordered them to 'find and retrieve'

the missing tanks, weapons and optical equipment, no matter how this was achieved!

Major-General Laner (who had been GOC, Northern Command during the 1967 Six Day War) was also called to his divisional headquarters on 6 October. Believing war would erupt at 18.00 hours, he was caught inspecting his division's mobilization progress when reports reached him that the Syrians had attacked. His division was totally unprepared for immediate combat and lacked the most basic communications and logistical elements. In response to the dire situation, he ordered the 'theft' of several APCs to co-ordinate his unit's activities. By 22.00 hours on 6 October all of Laner's staff officers were present at divisional headquarters, and 45 per cent of his units were equipped and ready for combat. Defence Minister Moshe Dayan personally ordered Laner to block all routes leading to the River Jordan. It was decided to split the Golan front, with UGDAT RAFUL responsible for all points north of the Bnot-Ya'akov-Kuneitra, UGDAT LANER all points south. Laner received two reserve brigades to command: Colonel Uri Orr's 679th, and Colonel Sarig's 17th. The brigades began to take up their combat positions along the Yehudia Road, and the Gamla Rise. The division advanced headquarters was established at the Arik Bridge, with Laner directing his forces as they arrived at the front.

The Syrians were fighting extremely well, and their armour and commando anti-tank teams were taking their toll of the Israeli tankers. The Syrian 47th and 51st Tank Brigades crossed the Tapline Route and headed towards the Gamla Rise through Yehudia. Colonel Sarig redeployed his forces and the Syrians attempted to outflank him by splitting their forces in two. The Syrian efforts were effective. While going head-on against Israeli armour, Syrian commando teams infiltrated behind Israeli positions, and engaged the Israeli tanks at suicidally close ranges with highly effective concentrated RPG fire. As a result, Israeli tank commanders were forced to spend as much time defending their rears, as directing fire against the oncoming tanks. One of the first units to reach Laner's advanced headquarters was the G'DUD SIYUR UGDATI (UGDAT RAFUL's reconnaissance battalion). Laner immediately incorporated them in to his own command, and rushed them to reinforce the outflanked 17th Armoured Brigade (Colonel Sarig had been

wounded, and the brigade command structure was in trouble) which was fighting for its life at the Kuzabia crossroads. Due to the extreme close range of the fighting, Laner was forced to direct the battle from the bridge, at company and even platoon level.

The Syrian 1st Armoured Division Commander, Colonel Tewfiq Jehani, concluded that nothing stood in the way of his crossing the River Jordan and advancing into Israel proper. The 1st Armoured Division even established a logistical and supply centre at Hushniya. In order to relieve the extreme pressure on UGDAT LANER in the Hushniya area, UGDAT MUSA's 205th Armoured Brigade was dispatched to attack the Syrian forces along the El Al – Rafid road, strangling their communications and supply lines. In co-ordination with the 205th Brigade's attack, UGDAT RAFUL's reconnaissance battalion, together with a lead battalion from the 17th Armoured Brigade, counter-attacked eastwards along the Yehudia approaches. Firing at long range, the Israeli tank gunners simply picked off the Syrian armour one by one. With long-range fire covering their advance, lead elements from the 17th Armoured Brigade advanced towards the Syrians, engaging them with close-range mobile tactics. Colonel Sarig's small force (approximately forty tanks) managed to destroy almost 150 Syrian tanks and vehicles. Although seriously wounded, Colonel Sarig continued to lead his men in the pitched battle, until 'forcefully' evacuated and replaced by a senior company commander. On hearing of Sarig's fate, the deputy commander of UGDAT LANER, Brigadier-General Moshe Bar-Kochba, took command of the area, leading the by now depleted units with great calm, skill and courage. Bar-Kochba, a large man, with an even larger aura of authority and leadership, had seen that most of his officers and tank commanders were either dead or wounded. Going from tank to tank, Bar-Kochba personally spoke to the crews, encouraging them and restoring their confidence. His presence had an astounding effect; the demoralized soldiers took stock of themselves and the situation. They rallied behind their commander.

Along the El-Al crossroads, Lieutenant-Colonel Mir was faced with the impossible task of holding the Syrian 132nd and 47th Armoured Brigades with a force of only eight M-51 Sherman tanks. Throughout the afternoon, the Syrians continued their efforts against Mir's tanks, but as night approached, and for no apparent reason, the Syrians stopped! Expecting an Israeli ambush, the Syrian commanders decided to wait for reinforcements and make their dash for the brigades at daybreak. This fatal pause gave the Israelis the crucial time needed to rush reservists to the front. Regrouped, UGDAT MUSA's brigades mounted a determined tank attack against the surprised Syrians. With the Syrians undergoing severe setbacks against the 7th Armoured Brigade in the north, and being contained in the south by the IDF reservists at the front, the tide had turned on the Golan.

## THE ORDER OF BRAVERY – THE SAGA OF THE 7TH ARMOURED BRIGADE

The 7th Armoured Brigade is truly one of the IDF's élite fighting units. One of the original seven brigades formed during the 1948 War of Independence, it had fought the Arab Legion at Latrun in the attempt to open the road to besieged Jerusalem. In 1956, under the command of Colonel Uri Ben-Ari (the father of IDF armoured warfare), the 7th Brigade had broken through the Egyptian defences in Sinai, reaching the Suez Canal in 100 hours. During the 1967 Six Day War the 7th Armoured Brigade smashed through the Egyptian line at Rafiah, and for the second time in ten years reached the Canal. In September 1973, troops both past and present from the 7th Armoured Brigade joined Brigade Commander Colonel Avigdor 'Yanush' Ben-Gal at an emotional 25th anniversary ceremony for the brigade at Latrun. In an impassioned speech Yanush stressed the brigade's proud heritage, and future challenge.

In 1973, the 7th Armoured Brigade consisted of two tank battalions: the 82nd, commanded by Lieutenant-Colonel Haim Barak, and Lieutenant-Colonel Kahalani's 77th (OZ) plus the 75th Mechanized Battalion commanded by Lieutenant-Colonel Yossi Eldar. Although stationed in southern Israel, the 7th Armoured Brigade had seen action in the north during security operations along the Golan and the Israeli-Lebanese frontier in the autumn of 1972. In the months prior to the hostilities, the 7th Armoured Brigade participated in one of the largest armoured manoeuvres in IDF history. The field exercise pitted 7th Armoured Brigade against determined defences, including anti-tank obstacles and minefields on the northern Golan. The exercise was a success; the 7th performed brilliantly. As tensions rose on the Golan in September 1973, 7th Armoured Brigade received orders to reinforce UGDAT RAFUL with one battalion, and Yanush sent his élite OZ or 77th Battalion, commanded by Lieutenant-Colonel Avigdor Kahalani. The 77th Battalion received tanks and supplies from the BARAK Brigade's emergency stores, and prepared itself for war. A forward command group reached the Golan to survey the area, with an M113 fitted with Intelligence-gathering equipment for Yanush, and a reconnaissance jeep for the battalion SAYERET (reconnaissance force). Yanush went over numerous contingency plans with Kahalani, while drills were performed round the clock to ensure quick mobilization from base camp to the defensive positions. Yanush wanted his men ready.

On 5 October, Armour Corps GOC, Major-General Bren Adan, ordered the entire 7th Armoured Brigade to join the 77th Battalion on the heights. The remaining portion of the brigade 'flew' north, reaching base in the early hours of the 6th. Joining them was a battalion made up of cadets from the IDF Armour School. Informed of war's imminence by Northern Command GOC, Major-General Hofi, Yanush raced towards his front-line units, studying the terrain with his officers, making sure everyone knew where their defensive positions were located. Yanush wanted everyone and everything ready for the expected Syrian 'evening' attack. By 13.00 hours, (twenty minutes before H-Hour) the situation was still a bit confused in the eventual make-up of UGDAT RAFUL. Units were still in transit as the 82nd Battalion of the 7th Armoured Brigade was integrated into BARAK, while BARAK's 74th Battalion, commanded, by Lieutenant-Colonel Yair Nofshi, was dispatched to the 7th. At 13.50, the Syrians opened up along the entire Golan.

The main objective for the 7th Armoured Brigade was a holding action: to secure the northern sector of the Golan and, in particular, to make sure that Syrian forces did not reach the strategic Kuneitra-Masada route. In this sector the Israelis possessed a major geographic defensive advantage. The anti-tank ditches, obstacles and defensive earth ramparts afforded the Israeli tanks maximum observation and protective firing positions. As the attack unfolded, the Syrian 7th and 9th Infantry Divisions' main thrust was against the area of MUTZAV 109, MUTZAV 105, and the area between Tel-Hermonit and 'Booster', the killing ground defended by the 77th Battalion. The Syrians attacked with huge tank forces advancing in parade formation supported by APCs and mechanized infantry. The moment the Syrians crossed the Purple Line tanks of the 7th Armoured Brigade opened fire at long range, but although suffering many losses, the Syrians continued their advance towards the Israeli positions. The 7th Armoured Brigade tank gunners, highly accurate at long range, had concentrated their fire on the Syrian tanks attempting to cross the minefields near the Purple Line. Although this accurate fire destroyed dozens of Syrian tanks, it was not enough to stop the flood of armour now heading towards the Israeli second line of defence, the anti-tank ditches. Yanush issued orders that all efforts must be made to destroy the MTU-55 bridgelayers, but the Syrians managed to get two bridges across, and the flood of Syrian armour continued to advance.

The 74th Battalion, commanded by Lieutenant-Colonel Yair Nofshi, was well positioned on 'Booster' Ridge near Tel-Hermonit. His forces came under intense artillery fire, which covered a major armoured advance in the valley below. Through the thick clouds of smoke, Nofshi was able to identify MTU-55s attempting to establish bridgeheads over the anti-tank ditch behind MUTZAV 107. He ordered all tanks under his command to concentrate fire on the bridgelayers, and at ranges of 2,000 yards managed to knock out all but two of the MTU-55s. Under massive tank, artillery and machine-gun fire, Syrian Combat Engineers bravely assisted the two vehicles to lay down their bridges. Two companies of tanks succeeded in crossing the bridges even though the 74th Battalion poured accurate fire into the killing ground. Lieutenant-Colonel Nofshi requested air support, but after watching one aircraft after another explode in mid-air as a result of surface-to-air missile fire, he decided against calling in any further aircraft. Dozens of destroyed Syrian tanks littered the valley below

'Booster', and two companies were sent in to destroy the bridges. Already in the first hours of the holding action reports flowed in of severe ammunition shortages, especially in the tank companies defending the MUTZAVIM. The Syrian tank onslaught continued virtually unmolested as the 7th Armoured Brigade did not receive adequate artillery support. As darkness fell on the battlefield, the Israeli shortage and Syrian abundance of night-fighting equipment became dangerously apparent. The Israeli tank

**Right:** Part of a Centurion company of Colonel Uri Orr's 679th Reserve Armoured Brigade prepares to move out against Syrian armour, 9 October 1973. (IDF Archives)

commanders, standing upright in their turrets in the thick of a murderous and continuous artillery barrage, found it most difficult to identify oncoming targets. The Syrians, equipped with a wide range of night-fighting optical and infra-red devices were able to turn night into day. Yanush ordered his support batteries to fire illumination shells, but the small supply available made them ineffective. Knowing that the Syrians would take full advantage of the situation, Yanush ordered his tanks to fire at anything moving in the darkness. By now the range had closed to 200 yards, and Syrian anti-tank commando teams had infiltrated the Israeli line, playing havoc with their deadly RPG-7s. Although the silhouettes outlined against blazing Syrian tanks in the valley below provided some visual target acquisition, the Israeli gunners had to improvize with flares, xenon lights projectors, and the seeking out of the telltale 'cat's eyes' characteristic of vehicles equipped with infra-red.

**Left:** A T-54, which failed to cross the anti-tank ditch, lies destroyed next to its bridging equipment. Many Syrian tanks and vehicles succeeded in crossing the ditch as a result of the bravery and determination of Syrian combat engineers. (IDF Archives)

As the battle ended at daylight on 7 October, the scene of destruction in the valley below, now visible to the Israeli tank crews, was fantastic. Hundreds of smouldering T-62, T-55/54 and Soviet-made APCs littered the killing ground between Tel-Hermonit and 'Booster'. The area became known to the soldiers of the 7th (as well as the world) as the 'Valley of Tears'. Most of the conscript soldiers had never seen combat before, and were numbed by the sight. The battle-hardened officers took advantage of the calm to take on fuel, ammunition, and grab a quick bite and smoke. At dawn the Syrian 78th Tank Brigade attempted once again to advance out of the

'Valley of Tears'. The exhausted Israelis managed to destroy dozens of Syrian tanks, but the waves of armour continued towards them. The Syrians attacked in such numbers that ranges of engagement varied from 10 to 3,000 yards. Most of the Israeli casualties were the tank commanders who courageously remained upright in their turrets. Unable to make substantial penetration, the Syrians withdrew at 13.00 hours, choosing to wait again until dark.

At 22.00 hours a reconnaissance jeep of the battalion SAYERET entered the 'Valley of Tears' on an Intelligence-gathering mission; their stealthy progress was disturbed by the deafening roar of a tank brigade on the move. Finding themselves in the centre of a major Syrian thrust, the jeep radioed their findings to Yanush, and gave their position so as not to be hit by the 7th's gunners who were preparing to fire from the ramps. Yanush gave the SAYERET recon paratroopers exactly five minutes to 'get their asses' back to base before opening fire. The Syrians attacked with the 3rd Armoured and 7th Infantry Divisions, led by units from the 81st Tank Brigade equipped entirely with T-62 tanks. At the 7th Armoured Brigade's disposal were only 35 tanks, many of them damaged from the previous day's fighting. Calmly, Yanush positioned his forces for battle, always making sure he had a force, no matter how small, in reserve. The accurate and continuous artillery barrage and tanks equipped with infra-red allowed the Syrians to close in on the Israelis, where the battle was now fought at ranges of less than thirty yards.

Throughout Monday, the 8th, Raful and Yanush contained the most difficult situation imaginable on the northern Golan. Composed and confident, they managed to bring some stability to the chaos and bolster the confidence of their men who by now felt they were fighting a losing battle. For on the 9th, the Syrians threw all they had at the 7th Armoured Brigade. Joining the Syrian 3rd Armoured and 7th Infantry Divisions in the latest assault was the Republican Guard equipped with T-62 tanks. Guardians of the Assad regime in Damascus, the Republican Guard had a reputation as fierce and fanatical soldiers (although their battlefield performance proved otherwise). Just south of Kuneitra, the 77th Battalion's 'Tiger Company', commanded by Captain Meir Zamir, was outflanked by a brigade-sized force which had entered the area

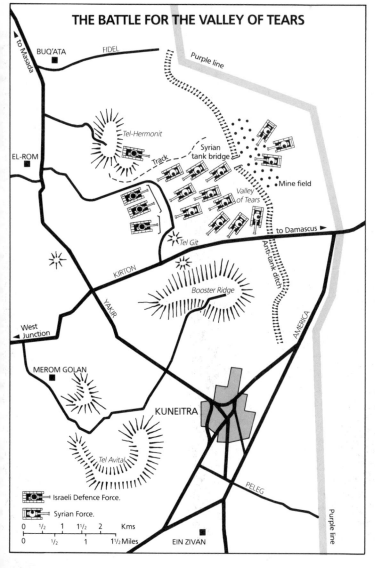

## THE BATTLE FOR THE VALLEY OF TEARS

to Masada
BUQ'ATA          FIDEL
Purple line
Tel-Hermonit
Track
EL-ROM
Syrian tank bridge
Valley of Tears
Mine field
to Damascus ►
Tel Git
Anti-tank ditch
KIRTON
Booster Ridge
YAKIR
AMERICA
West Junction
MEROM GOLAN
KUNEITRA
Tel Avital
PELEG
Israeli Defence Force.
Syrian Force.
Purple line
0   ½   1   1½   2   Kms
0       ½       1       1½ Miles
EIN ZIVAN

**Right:** The 'Valley of Tears', 8 October 1973. 'Bewildered' Syrian T-62s attempt to regroup in the shadows of destroyed tanks in the anti-tank ditch near Tel-Git. (IGPO)

under the cover of darkness. 'Tiger Company' had only seven tanks at its disposal, but managed to hold off two companies of infantry and destroy more than thirty tanks. Later that night 'Tiger Company' succeeded in outflanking a tank force attacking 'Booster'. Although blind without night-fighting equipment, Captain Zamir managed to maul the Syrian force, leaving twenty burning T-55s without suffering a single casualty. The men of the 7th Armoured Brigade had by now reached the limit of their endurance. They had been fighting non-stop for three days and two nights. There was no time to eat, sleep, or do anything else except fight and survive. Already 76 men of the brigade had fallen in action, many of them officers. There were only 32 operational tanks remaining of the 105 that had begun the battle three days earlier. The brigade's heroic ordnance crews worked feverishly to repair damaged tanks which they themselves had retrieved under fire. Yanush dispatched a reserve force of

five tanks half a mile behind his forward defensive lines as a last resort in case the Syrians succeeded in a breakthrough.

The Syrian attack at 08.00 hours on 9 October was the most ferocious the Israelis had yet experienced. In addition to the thousands of artillery shells and Katyusha rockets slamming the Israeli positions, the Syrians launched air-strikes against the tank forces on the ramps. Seven Mi-8 helicopters attempted to land a commando force near Buq'ata, but only four of

them managed to land, with one Mi-8 shot down by an HE round fired from a Centurion's 105mm gun. At the same time, a small force from the SAYERET HATIVATIT (7th Armoured Brigade's reconnaissance unit), commanded by Captain Uri Karshani, was in the area of Buq'ata, evacuating wounded soldiers from the GOLANI Brigade. By now the Syrians had dug in, waiting in ambush for the approaching recon unit. The Syrians opened up with small arms and RPG fire, damaging the lead SAYERET

**Right:** A Centurion crew grabs a quick bite following the battle for the 'Valley of Tears'. (IDF Archives)

tank. The ensuing fire-fight developed into a vicious hand-to-hand battle. A wounded GOLANI soldier managed to reach the blazing tank's .50 calibre turret-mounted machine-gun, and opened fire. The surviving Syrian commando force dispersed. The SAYERET suffered very heavy losses, but by being in the right place at the right time they had destroyed a serious anti-tank threat to the 7th Armoured Brigade.

Back along the 7th Armoured Brigade's defensive lines, the blistering Syrian bombardment continued without let-up. Yanush observed a Syrian tank force, 100 strong, advance towards his lines, and told Raful that this was going to be the turning-point on the front. Yanush ordered his exhausted men to acquire targets and fire, destroying a large number of Syrian tanks at maximum range. As the Syrians closed in, the artillery barrage on the 77th Battalion increased in intensity, and began to take its toll of the tank commanders standing upright in their turrets. Realizing that his already exhausted tank crews were becoming quite ineffective as a result of the Syrian pressure, Kahalani requested permission from Yanush to withdraw 400 yards from the ramps. Permission was granted, and as Kahalani's tank force (now numbering only six vehicles) withdrew, the Syrians quickly captured the ramp's crest, enveloping the 77th Battalion in the process. At the same time, Captain Zamir's 'Tiger Company' had its hands full fighting off a combined Syrian infantry and armour attack on Tel Git on the main Damascus road just north of 'Booster'. Captain Zamir's tanks were now down to only two rounds per tank.

As the battle raged, Kahalani found the remnants of his battalion fighting Syrian armour on all sides. Tanks were shooting at one another from point-blank range. Noticing that his tank was surrounded by four Syrian tanks, Kahalani ordered his gunner to fire rapidly, and in the space of ninety seconds four T-62s were set ablaze. The Syrians fought tenaciously, running wildly about looking for new tanks to replace their own damaged ones. They earned the respect of the Israeli soldiers who had once held them in contempt. The Syrian infiltration of the Israeli positions was now complete; the 7th Armoured Brigade was surrounded. Fighting at point-blank range on a 360° radius, command control now became impossible. On both sides individual tanks were fighting alone, in hundreds of private battles. Yanush had feared that this was the end, and that the 7th was to suffer the same fate as his friend Ben-Shoham's BARAK Brigade. His men were utterly exhausted, fighting instinctively, not realizing the desperation of their plight. With his officers barely conscious, Yanush radioed Raful informing him of the brigade's situation, apologetically stating that he wasn't sure if he could hold on. Knowing that the 7th Armoured Brigade

was all that stood in the way of a Syrian push towards the River Dan and Kiryat Shmoneh, Raful urged Yanush to 'hold on just thirty minutes longer', telling him that reinforcements would be arriving shortly.

On its way to the 7th Armoured Brigade's rescue were the remnants of the BARAK Brigade, thirteen tanks in all, led by Lieutenant-Colonel Yossi Ben-Hanan (until two weeks earlier, 53rd Battalion's commander). Yanush

**Right:** A Centurion receives an emergency overhaul from mobile ordnance near MUTZAV 110. (IDF Archives)

and Ben-Hanan were firm friends, rising through the ranks of the Armour Corps together. In fact, during their stint at the IDF Armour Command College, the two had opted to write numerous papers on armour strategy rather than go on leave. On Yom Kippur, Ben-Hanan was enjoying an adventurous honeymoon deep in the Himalayas. Making his way back to Israel as quickly as possible, Ben-Hanan collected his gear at Lod Airport and raced towards the Golan. On Tuesday, 9 October, he reached Major-General Hofi's headquarters and learned of BARAK Brigade's situation. Taking command of the remnants, Ben-Hanan was ordered to reinforce the beleaguered 7th Armoured Brigade. Led by BARAK Brigade's operations officer riding shotgun in a jeep, Ben-Hanan raced towards the northern sector with the thirteen surviving BARAK tanks. 7th Armoured Brigade was by now near total

**Left:** Men of Captain Meir Zamir's 'Tiger Company' examine operational charts during a break in the fighting. The fatigue of battle is clearly evident on the men's faces. (IDF Archives)

**Right:** Lieutenant-Colonel Avigdor Kahalani (right), commander of 7th Armoured Brigade's 77th Battalion during a break in the fighting, 9 October 1973. It was his brilliant leadership that prevented the northern Golan from being overrun. (IDF Archives)

annihilation; only seven tanks were operational, and 'Tiger Company' had run out of ammunition. Ben-Hanan's rescue force immediately raced up 'Booster' ridge and engaged Syrian armour at point-blank range, destroying more than 22 tanks. The arrival of Ben-Hanan caused the Syrians to lose heart. They had fought themselves to a standstill, and the arrival of fresh troops was the last straw. An hour after Ben-Hanan entered the battle, reports came in from the besieged MUTZAV 107 that the Syrian supply columns were retreating. As the beaten tank units withdrew, Israeli artillery harried their wake, even firing captured Katyusha rockets at their former owners. Syrian offensive capabilities in the northern Golan had been crushed. A very proud and relieved Raful patched into the 7th Armoured Brigade's communications network, and told his men 'You have saved the people of Israel.'

The tank crews began to disembark from their vehicles and survey the utter destruction around them. Most of the surviving troops of the brigade were wounded, many were shell-shocked and all were completely exhausted. The 7th Armoured Brigade's defence of the northern Golan has become an epic in IDF folklore. Credit for the victory is shared equally by all who fought and won against such insurmountable odds. The conscripts, many of whom were only eighteen years old, had trained hard and long in this élite unit, and proved their worth in a situation no combat simulator could ever duplicate. Lying silently below in the 'Valley of Tears' were the remains of more than 500 Syrian tanks and vehicles, their presence a testament to the determination and bravery of the Syrian tank soldier, and to the men of the 7th Armoured Brigade who managed to stop them.

## GUNSIGHTS ON DAMASCUS – THE ISRAELI COUNTER-ATTACK

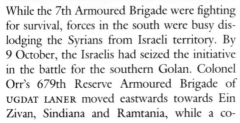

While the 7th Armoured Brigade were fighting for survival, forces in the south were busy dislodging the Syrians from Israeli territory. By 9 October, the Israelis had seized the initiative in the battle for the southern Golan. Colonel Orr's 679th Reserve Armoured Brigade of UGDAT LANER moved eastwards towards Ein Zivan, Sindiana and Ramtania, while a co-ordinated effort was undertaken by Colonel Sarig's 17th Armoured Brigade through the Kuzabia crossroads along the Tapline Route towards the Syrian supply and logistics centre at Hushniya. The Syrians swiftly organized defensive points and put up a stubborn resistance, dozens of Israeli tanks were hit, and the attrition among officers (especially at company command level) became alarming. The attacking Israeli forces were greatly assisted in their efforts by the IAF which, after dealing with the vast Syrian SAM umbrella, entered the battle in a ground-support role. The air strikes halted Syrian ammunition and fuel supply efforts, as

**Right:** A knocked out Centurion stands at the side of the road near MUTZAV 107. The tank belonged to a deputy company commander (Hebrew lettering located right, below depressed gun barrel). Note Syrian BTR-60 in background. (IDF Archives)

well as destroying large numbers of tanks and vehicles.

In the south, UGDAT MUSA's 4th Reserve Armoured Brigade, commanded by Colonel Ya'akov 'Pepper' Hadar, and the 9th Reserve Armoured Brigade, commanded by Colonel Mordechai Ben-Porat, mounted a major counter-attack against the Syrian 9th Infantry Division along the El Al route towards Rafid. The attack went badly for the Israelis, and Colonel Yossi Peled's 205th Armoured Brigade had to be called up. The advance was slow and costly, the Israelis facing heavy opposition on both flanks. The Syrians responded with heavy

artillery fire, slowing the Israeli advance. In the end, 205th Armoured Brigade managed to retake Ramat Magshimim, and although equipped with antiquated M-51 Shermans, managed to destroy most of the Syrian force (more than 63 tanks were found abandoned). The 205th Armoured Brigade continued its advance against fanatical Syrian resistance. In the area of Tel-Saki, a Syrian anti-tank battalion with Sagger-equipped BRDM APCs (and antiquated Su-100s as well) was sent in to reinforce the 132nd Brigade, and this force fired more than *thirty* Sagger anti-tank missiles at the oncoming Israelis. Attempting to capture Tel

**Right:** A knocked out Syrian BTR-60 by the side of the road leading to Sindiana, 10 October 1973. (IDF Archives)

**Far right:** A Centurion damaged by an anti-tank mine receives emergency care at a mobile ordnance base. (IDF Archives)

**Right:** On the road to Damascus, 10 October 1973. (IDF Archives)

Kudne, the 9th Brigade attacked the Syrian 40th Mechanized Brigade in a vicious close-quarter battle. Although suffering heavy losses, UGDAT MUSA continued to apply heavy pressure on the Syrians at Tel Kudne and Tel Fazra; while a co-ordinated effort by the 679th and 17th Armoured Brigades attempted to cut off the Hushniya crossroads, where the Syrians had a strong concentration of forces. With UGDAT MUSA applying pressure from the south and UGDAT LANER from the north, the 'Hushniya Pocket' was turned into a tank killing ground comparable in magnitude to the 'Valley of Tears'. Two entire Syrian brigades were decimated in the Hushniya Pocket, and hundreds of destroyed tanks, APCs, guns, and supply vehicles dotted the area.

Throughout 10 October, the Israelis mopped up any pockets of Syrian resistance inside the Purple Line. That same day, Iraq formally entered the war. It mobilized its armed forces, transferred 100 MiGs to air bases in western Iraq, and sent upwards of 18,000 troops and 350 tanks towards the Golan. Jordan entered the war as well, by reluctantly sending their élite 40th Armoured Brigade to Syria. The

Soviet Union urged other Arab states to commit forces and do their 'obligated Arab duty'.

The question of whether or not to invade Syria was considered at a late night General Staff meeting at the BOR (the underground command and control centre at IDF GHQ in Tel Aviv) on 10 October. Defence Minister Moshe Dayan was against pushing into Syria proper, fearing Soviet military intervention (Cuban forces were already in Syria). Ever cognizant of the lack of strategic depth available to the forces on the Golan (as opposed to the geographic leverage still enjoyed by the embattled Israelis in Sinai), Chief of Staff Lieutenant-General David 'Dado' Elazar favoured total destruction of Syrian offensive capabilities by moving 22 kilometres inside Syria. Timing of the counter-attack was also crucial, since the Soviet effort to resupply Syria was fully under way, and the General Staff feared that the absorption of the weaponry would dictate events on the battlefield. Prime Minister Golda Meir agreed with her Chief of Staff, and sanctioned the counter-attack for 11 October. Major-General Hofi decided to launch the counter-attack in the northern sector since it constituted the shortest route towards Damascus, and to diminish the possibilities of a Syrian counter outflanking movement, since the impassable Mount Hermon area was on UGDAT RAFUL's left flank. The counter-attack was to be led by UGDAT RAFUL along the Tel Shams-Mazrat Beit Jan route. The UGDAT RAFUL attack would act as cover for UGDAT LANER's push along the heavily fortified Kuneitra-Damascus highway. Major-General Hofi decided that should UGDAT LANER become bogged down, it was to follow UGDAT RAFUL's advance. Should the push succeed, UGDAT RAFUL would follow in support. UGDAT MUSA was to be held in reserve, protecting the rear flank and clearing up remaining Syrian pockets still inside the Purple Line. H-Hour for UGDAT RAFUL was 11.00 hours, with UGDAT LANER's push to follow two hours later.

Leading UGDAT RAFUL's advance was the 7th Armoured Brigade, which spent the whole of 10 October feverishly re-fitting and re-equipping. The 7th Armoured Brigade was now rein-

forced to include the 77th Battalion under Kahalani, the remnants of Lieutenant-Colonel Yair Nofshi's 74th Battalion, Lieutenant-Colonel Ben-Hanan's BARAK Brigade survivors, as well as KOACH AMOS, a reinforced reserve tank battalion under the command of Lieutenant-Colonel Amos Katz. Only one day after being on the verge of destruction, Yanush was able to field an impressive force of four fully equipped tank battalions. Yanush split his forces in two, with the 77th and KOACH AMOS Battalions to capture Hader and Mazrat Beit Jan, the remaining forces to seize Jubata, the Khan Arnaba Heights, the vast Syrian military installations at Hales, and Tel Shams. The 7th Armoured Brigade command briefing at 23.00 hours on 10 October was a highly emotional gathering. Seated before Yanush was a group of soldiers who had been on the brink of annihilation only 24 hours earlier. They had fought continuously for 96 hours under the most adverse conditions. They had lost many of their officers and friends, and they were exhausted. Men who had not slept since the outbreak of

**Right:** A Centurion (unidentified unit) searches the road for Syrian armour, 11 October 1973. (IDF Archives)

**Opposite page, top:** During the counter-attack, one of Lieutenant-Colonel Ben-Hanan's Centurions advances towards destroyed Syrian T-55s. The Hebrew sign at left is an exercise marker which reads 'DANGER-FIRING ZONE-SHOOTING IN THE AREA'. (IDF Archives)

**Opposite page, bottom:** A M48 AVLB Bridgelayer thirteen kilometres inside Syria. The M48 AVLBs were utilized in much the same way as their Syrian MTU-55 counterparts were, to cross anti-tank obstacles in heavily defended areas. (IDF Archives)

the war were now expected to lead a major counter-attack against a still capable enemy. As Yanush addressed them, the emotions held in check during the holding actions expressed themselves, as every order and unit directive brought back memories of friends who had fallen. Yanush informed Raful and Major-General Hofi that his men were ready.

Speed of breakout was crucial. The route was heavily wooded, surrounded by minefields, and anti-tank defences on the Syrian side of the Purple Line. At 11.00 hours on 11 October, under cover of heavy air and artillery attacks, 7th Armoured Brigade crossed the Purple Line into Syria. The 77th Tank Battalion and KOACH AMOS picked their way through the minefields, and attacked the Syrian 7th Infantry Division's 68th Infantry Brigade. After many difficulties in negotiating the rocky terrain, the 77th Battalion and KOACH AMOS managed to reach the Hader crossroads unmolested. Moving on to Mazrat Beit Jan, it was held back by a determined co-ordinated Syrian air, armour, and artillery effort. The Syrians counter-attacked, attempting to outflank the 77th Battalion from the north, and KOACH AMOS from the east. Heavy fighting ensued for six hours without let-up in the village, and tank fought tank at point-blank range in a built-up area. On

12 October after suffering heavy losses, Mazrat Beit Jan was in Israeli hands.

Lieutenant-Colonel Ben-Hanan led his BARAK Brigade survivors and the 82nd Battalion across the Purple Line into Syria. BARAK Brigade had lost 90 per cent of its officers during the battles in the south, and only a few of the original company commanders remained. Fighting on the Tel Ahmar high ground, Ben-Hanan's force faced stubborn Sagger anti-tank missile defences. Many tanks were hit by the 'invisible' Sagger teams making excellent use of the terrain as cover. Late in the evening of 11 October, 82nd Battalion cap-

tured the Druze hamlet of Horfa, while Ben-Hanan's force was busy in its attempt to capture the Maatz crossroads. A Syrian MiG attack wounded Ben-Hanan seriously, but he refused to be evacuated. Yanush ordered Ben-Hanan to move up towards the hills surrounding the Tel Shams-Damascus road junction, but the three attempts his battalion made to reach the area were beaten off by Sagger companies. The determined defences, and the impassable terrain halted the advance, all attempts to regroup and attack ended in failure.

In the meantime Yanush established 7th Armoured Brigade's forward headquarters at

**Right:** An M-51 races towards the front line inside Syria, 13 October 1973. Note searchlight fitted near turret-mounted .50 calibre machine-gun. With Syrian commando anti-tank teams operating mainly at night, IDF armour positions needed maximum night identification capabilities. (IDF Archives)

**Opposite page:** A recon paratrooper from UGDAT RAFUL's G'DUD SIYUR (recon battalion) carefully checks out a damaged Syrian BRDM abandoned near Tel Shams. Note Sagger missiles in firing position. (IDF Archives)

Hales, and after meeting his top officers, concluded that it would require a full brigade effort to take Tel Shams. All through the night of the 12th, the friends Yanush and Ben-Hanan studied maps, aerial photographs, and surveyed the area through field glasses. Yanush concluded that, given the hostile terrain and dominant defensive positions on the approaches to Tel Shams, any attack had only a 50 per cent chance of succeeding. Ben-Hanan promptly volunteered to lead. Ben-Hanan's Battalion was composed of twenty tanks and vehicles divided into two companies. From his command post at Hales, Yanush observed Ben-

Hanan's force advance slowly and cautiously towards Tel Shams. Ten of his tanks were suddenly destroyed in an ambush. Ben-Hanan decided to storm Tel Shams from the rear, and with a supporting artillery barrage, began to climb up the Tel's slope. Suddenly, Sagger teams, hiding behind volcanic boulders, opened fire, destroying four of the six tanks. Ben-Hanan was himself seriously wounded, and had to be rescued in a daring night operation conducted by Brigade SAYERET commanded by Captain Yonatan 'Yoni' Netanyahu (Yoni was awarded the OT HAMOFET bravery medal for this operation, and was killed three years later

**Right:** A Centurion patrol at the outskirts of Kuneitra on 28 October 1973. Although the cease-fire of 24 October held firm, small though deadly fire-fights were common in a war of attrition lasting well into 1974. (IGPO)

leading the commando raid at Entebbe). Distraught by his friend's serious wounds, Yanush realized that an armour assault on Tel Shams was a serious error. In fact, Raful ordered a battalion from 31st Parachute Brigade to take Tel Shams, and on the 13th, it was captured at the expense of only four wounded.

UGDAT LANER broke out across the Purple Line on the Damascus Road with 679th Reserve Armoured Brigade deployed to cover 17th Armoured Brigade. Colonel Sarig had been seriously wounded in the fighting days earlier on the Yehudia Road, and now returned to his command, bandages and all. The 17th Armoured Brigade's SAYERET HATIVATIT led the attack, but accurate Syrian artillery fire slowed the advance to a crawl. As the unit attempted to regroup, Syrian commandos with RPGs and Saggers opened fire, devastating the recon force. In an hour, more than 25 of the brigade's tanks and vehicles were in flames. Major-General Laner decided to evacuate 17th Armoured Brigade, which was now caught in vicious anti-tank crossfire. The 679th Reserve Armoured Brigade was sent in as reinforcements, but they too found themselves in a murderous killing ground. The deeper the Israelis advanced into Syria, the more fanatical the defence became. The armour war on the Golan had changed, since it was now tank against missile. IDF armoured efforts were achieving the minimum results at maximum cost. A new strategy was necessary if the push into Syria were to succeed. It was decided to send in infantry and paratroop battalions against the missile defences in order to secure the routes of advance.

With forces advancing on her capital, and a successful air attack on General Staff HQ, the Syrian posture of confidence crumbled. In an act of desperation, the Syrians fired FROG surface-to-surface missiles at Migdal Ha'emek and Kibbutz Geva in the Galilee. Undaunted, the Israelis continued to advance. On 12 October UGDAT LANER advanced, by-passing Tel Maschara and capturing the village of Nasej. Major-General Laner consolidated his flanks, with 9th Brigade reaching Tel el-Mal, on its route towards Knacker. The Syrians were now on the run. At this point, forces of the Iraqi 3rd Armoured Division advanced on the Great Leja Plain towards IDF positions at Knacker and those threatening the Kiswe army barracks west of Damascus. Moving in parade formation, the 'shinny' Iraqi tanks were allowed to close to within 300 yards of IDF lines, before tanks of 679th Reserve Armoured Brigade opened fire. Seventeen Iraqi tanks were destroyed immediately and the advance was stemmed. Expecting a fresh Iraqi attack, Laner deployed his forces in box formation. The 9th Reserve Armoured Brigade was deployed in the foothills of Tel Sha'ar, 679th Reserve Armoured Brigade near Nasej, 17th Armoured Brigade deployed at a point between the 9th and 679th Brigades, while 205th Armoured Brigade sat along the Tel Maschara-Jaba road.

At 21.00 hours on the 12th, the Iraqis moved into the Israeli trap. With every divisional gun aiming at the approaching Iraqis, Laner eagerly waited for the range to close in and issued the order to fire. As the Iraqis entered deeper into the trap, the guns of 9th Reserve Armoured Brigade's Sherman and Centurion tanks opened fire. Within minutes, eighty Iraqi tanks were in flames, with *no* Israeli casualties. It was the first armour battle for the Iraqis in their military history, and in a matter of seconds two brigades were lost. The 205th Armoured Brigade then raced to capture Tel Maschara and Tel Nasej. The next day, 9th Reserve Armoured Brigade captured the strategic heights at Tel Antar, and Tel el-Alakieh. Exhausted and with ammunition shortages the Israelis were ordered to halt.

On 16 October, the Jordanian 40th Armoured Brigade (protecting the Syrian 5th Infantry Division's flank) attacked positions held by UGDAT LANER. Ironically, 40th Armoured Brigade had decimated the Syrian 5th Infantry Division three years earlier during the Syrian invasion of Jordan in 'Black September' 1970. The 40th Armoured Brigade advanced towards Tel Maschara, where 17th Armoured Brigade awaited them. Twenty-eight Jordanian tanks were destroyed in the mêlée and the attack was disrupted. The inter-army co-operation attempted between the Syrians, Iraqis and Jordanians failed miserably, with ally firing on ally. The IDF consolidated its lines and Damascus was brought within artillery range. It was decided against entering Damascus itself, for the IDF was unwilling to risk the heavy losses that the capturing of a major Arab capital city would entail.

On 17 October, Major-General Peled relieved an exhausted and fatigued Laner. Major-General Laner had led his reservist forces brilliantly and brought them within grasp of a major historical victory. Between 17 and 22 October, remnants of the Syrian 1st Armoured Division together with the Jordanian 40th Armoured Brigade and the Iraqi 3rd Armoured Division mounted daily attacks against Israeli positions. These ineffectual and unco-ordinated attacks commenced daily between 10.00 and 11.00 hours, and Israeli forces had no difficulty holding the line. The most serious of these attacks occurred on 20 October, with the Syrians, Iraqis, and Jordanians losing well over 120 tanks in a seven-hour battle. Two days later, a combined attack of heli-borne paratroopers and GOLANI infantrymen recaptured Mount Hermon after a

**Right:** At the wrong end of the deadly 105mm gun! A Centurion crew on patrol within Syrian territory, searches for Syrian or 'Cuban' tanks, November 1973. Although demoralized somewhat by over 2 months at the front under constant combat stress, IDF tank crews operated in a highly professional and effective manner throughout their mobilized period 'up north'. (IDF Spokesman)

savage close-quarter battle. That day, both the Israelis and Syrians accepted a UN-sponsored ceasefire, and the war on the Golan was over.

Although a war of attrition would continue on the Golan well into 1974, with daily artillery and tank duels (the Israelis even encountered Cuban armoured forces!), the front remained stable until the IDF withdrew to the Purple Line. The war had cost the Syrians 3,612 dead, 6,900 wounded and, the pride of her armoured forces, 1,500 tanks destroyed. Israeli losses were also high, with 772 killed, 2,453 wounded and 250 tanks knocked out, of which 150 were repaired and returned to active service. Victory was achieved as a result of the determination, bravery and dedication of the

Israeli tank soldier for whom no personal sacrifice was too great. Fifty-three armour soldiers were awarded the three IDF medals for valour, many of them posthumously. Recipients of the highest order, OT HAGVURA (Order of Bravery), included Captain Tzvi Tzvicka Greengold and Lieutenant-Colonel Avigdor Kahalani. Those awarded OT HA'OZ (Order of Courage) and OT HAMOFET (Order of Exemplary Service) medals included Lieutenant-Colonel Ben-Hanan, Colonel Ben-Shoham, Major Meir Zamir, Lieutenant-Colonel Yair Nofshi, Lieutenant-Colonel Yosef Eldar, and 45 others, from Colonels to Privates. These truly remarkable men, true heroes of Israel, had saved the nation.

# 1973
# THE YOM KIPPUR WAR IN SINAI

The vast desert regions of Sinai, where Moses received the Ten Commandments and from where the Children of Israel entered the land of Canaan has always had a special significance in the history and heritage of the Jewish Nation. The Sinai peninsula is 134 miles long on the Mediterranean coast, 311 miles long from the Mediterranean banks of the Suez Canal to the Gulf of Suez, and 155 miles long from the Gulf of Aqaba, in the east, to Suez. The Suez Canal is some 200 yards wide, and 200 miles long from Port Said on the Mediterranean to Suez in

the Red Sea. A barrier between Egypt and Israel, the IDF captured Sinai in a 100-hour dash during 'MIVTZA KADESH', the 1956 Suez War. Although returned to Egypt a year later, it was once again seized in a lightning strike during the 1967 Six Day War. This time Israel refused to return Sinai, holding it as a bargaining chip in hoped for peace negotiations. Egyptian President, Gamal Abdel Nasser, saw the Israeli presence in Sinai as a dastardly symbol of Egyptian humiliation, and vowed to retrieve it at all costs. In the 1,000-day War of

**Above:** A MA'GACHIM M-60 prepares to move out hours before the Egyptian blitz, 6 October 1973. (IDF Archives)

**Right:** A Centurion explodes in a flaming ball after being hit by a Sagger missile fired by Egyptian commando anti-tank teams near Drora, 6 October 1973. (IDF Archives)

Attrition (1967–70), the Egyptians applied intense military pressure on IDF forces in Sinai with incessant artillery bombardments and commando raids. These actions only strengthened Israeli resolve to remain in Sinai, and by 1972, Egyptian President, Anwar es-Sadat, concluded that the only way the Israelis could be ousted from Sinai was by full-scale war.

As a result of the constant Egyptian artillery pressure, 33 fortified outposts (together with numerous second-line positions) were constructed between 1968 and 1971 along the entire length of the Suez Canal; although only sixteen of them remained operational by 1973. They were positioned 5–7 miles from one another, each one responsible for ½ to 1 mile on each flank. Each MAOZ (fortification) was defended by an infantry platoon, with covering tank and artillery forces positioned on defensive earth ramparts overlooking the canal. Points between fortifications were covered by mechanized patrols and forward observation posts. Connecting the MAOZIM ran the LEXICON road, supported by a parallel road five miles east inland called the 'Artillery Road' which allowed SP guns to move rapidly between the MAOZIM. The entire area was served by an extensive network of criss-crossing roads, which provided maximum mobility for reinforcements bound for the front, and in the event of war provided pre-staging areas for counter-attacking forces. The entire system became known as the Bar-Lev Line, named after then IDF Chief of Staff, Lieutenant-General Haim Bar-Lev. Never intended to be the Israeli 'Maginot Line'; the Bar-Lev Line's purpose was to force an attack into pre-designated areas, when any advance could be held until reinforcements and reservists could arrive. For maximum effectiveness, it was crucial that the MAOZIM receive adequate advance warning of any impending attack. In case of war, the positions could only hold out with close air, armour, and artillery support.

Military responsibility for the 37,000 square miles of Sinai (as well as the southern portion of Israel) lay with IDF, Southern Command. In July 1973, Major-General Shmuel 'Gorodish' Gonen was appointed GOC, Southern Command, replacing the maverick and ever-controversial Major-General Ariel 'Arik' Sharon, of UNIT 101 and 202nd Paratroop Brigade fame (who retired from active service and was given command of Gonen's former reserve division in Southern Command). Gonen, a highly decorated armour officer, had led 7th Armoured Brigade to victory during the 1967 War in Sinai. Although a fearless and capable field commander, Gonen was a fanatical disciplinarian, and tended to have difficulty with the men in his command. One of his first priorities as GOC, Southern Command was the construction of tank ramps along the Bar-Lev Line's *second* line of defence, enabling tanks to engage forces crossing the canal at long ranges. The Egyptians had raised the banks on their side of the canal to 130 feet which enabled them to look down on the Bar-Lev Line and peer into the second-line defences. Gonen responded by authorizing earthworks which camouflaged activity behind the MAOZIM. In addition, other defences were re-examined, including oil pipelines stored under the MAOZIM. Should the Egyptians stage a crossing, the tanks would spray ignited oil into the canal, turning it into a sea of flames. The system was neglected by Southern Command, and although attempts to revive it were attempted, it was too late.

Egypt possessed a standing army of enormous size. Its total strength included 800,000 troops, 2,200 tanks, 2,300 artillery pieces, more than 150 SAM batteries, and 550 combat aircraft. Crossing the canal had been an Egyptian obsession since 1967, and the planning for the operation was thought out down to the smallest detail. Egyptian Minister of War and Joint Arab Armies Commander-in-Chief, General Ismail, and Egyptian Chief of Staff, General Sa'ad es-Dinn Shazli, knew that in order *not* to repeat the folly of 1967, every aspect of the attack had to be perfected. Training for the operation was conducted day in and day out, with nothing left to chance. Realizing that once across the canal their main vulnerability lay with exposed armour formations at the mercy of IAF air attack, an effective mobile SAM umbrella screen was put in place.

The Egyptian attack force was divided in two. Responsibility for the northern sector of the front, from Port Said to Fayid in the middle of the Great Bitter Lakes, lay with the Egyptian Second Army. It consisted of the 18th Infantry Division, the 2nd Infantry Division, and the 16th Infantry Division. The Third Army, responsible for the southern sector of the attack consisted of the 7th Infantry Divi-

sion, and the 19th Infantry Division. Each infantry division was supported by an armoured brigade. In addition, each army had a second echelon consisting of armour and mechanized divisions. Supporting the two army groups were two paratroop brigades, 28 commando battalions, and a marine brigade. The first phase, Operation 'Badr' (the Egyptian code-name for the crossing), was to take place between 6 and 9 October. Ten bridges were to be set in place across the canal. H-Hour for the Egyptian blitz was 13.45 hours, 6 October 1973.

## HOLDING THE LINE – UGDAT ALBERT

The Egyptian attack came as no surprise to Major-General Avraham 'Albert' Mandler, commander of UGDAT ALBERT, the regular armoured division stationed along the canal line. The impending signs of attack were only too obvious to the division's senior officers, and attempts to have the division placed on full alert were under way. Prior to the Egyptian attack on 6 October, UGDAT ALBERT consisted of three armoured brigades with a total of 290 tanks: 401st Armoured Brigade, equipped with M-60 Patton tanks under the command of Colonel Dan Shomron, 14th Armoured Brigade commanded by Colonel Amnon Reshef, and 460th Armoured Brigade, commanded by Gabi Amir. When Albert ordered Colonel Amir to ready his forces for war, Amir argued that mobilization steps were unnecessary since the Egyptians 'lacked' the courage to cross the canal. The Bar-lev Line MAOZIM were 'supposed' to be manned by crack infantry units, but many of these men were on ROSH HASHANA (New Year) leave. Instead, the line was held by ill-trained reservists from a brigade made up of Jerusalem residents. Junior Intelligence officers at Southern Command had uncovered Egyptian intentions including exact time of attack and disposition of forces; yet reports sent to their superiors were dismissed, even ignored. Even as late as 5 October, A'MAN Chief, Major-General Eliezer 'Eli' Zeira, was still convinced that war was unlikely. As a result, most of the regular infantry units were not returned to their posts. Israel's most impor-

**Right:** A modified M-48 takes on fuel, ammunition and water during a brief respite at Lituf, 7 October 1973. (IDF Archives)

tant defensive line was held by only 436 reservists!

The Egyptian attack along the entire length of the Suez Canal was unprecedented in its ferocity. A total of 240 MiG, Sukhoi and Tupelov aircraft attacked Hawk SAM batteries along the length of the front, the command nerve centre at Refidim, and the northernmost MAOZ at BUDAPEST east of Port Fuad. At the same time, 2,000 guns of all calibres opened up on the MAOZIM, while tanks waiting to be ferried across the canal fired point-blank into Bar-Lev Line positions just across the water-way. Long-range FROG missiles were fired at IDF military installations at Tasa and Refidim. 175 shells per second rained down on the MAOZIM and rear positions in a barrage lasting 53 minutes with over *3,000* tons of ammunition being fired. At 14.15 hours specially trained Egyptian infantrymen, paddling furiously in rubber dinghies, began crossing the canal. High sand barriers on the Israeli side of the canal were ingeniously removed by the Egyptians using high-powered hoses. In areas under attack by the Second Army, the hoses

disintegrated the sand walls in minutes; while in the Third Army's area the hoses created an impassable labyrinth of mud. Naval commando and special force teams landed first, isolating the MAOZIM; while 8,000 infantrymen of the first wave (crossing in teams of twelve) made their way across the canal in rubber dinghies. Heading eastwards, the first wave avoided bogging down and by-passed the MAOZIM to establish a beach-head some two miles deep. Commando anti-tank teams equipped with RPG-7s and Sagger missiles landed right behind the first wave. They mined the tank ramparts, and prepared ambushes against the expected IDF armour reinforcements.

Egyptian estimates of casualties during the crossing had been placed as high as 30–40 per cent, and the Egyptian High Command had forbidden military photographers to accompany the forces crossing the canal (all the photographs were taken days later in more 'secure' and 'dramatic' surroundings). But the Egyptian attack was so well planned and executed, that only 208 men were killed during the actual crossing. The beleaguered Israeli

defenders attempted in vain to hold off the Egyptians whose commanders were amazed to see individual Israeli tanks confronting entire brigades of infantry equipped with a wide array of anti-tank weaponry. The major Egyptian setback of the day, however, came with their commando anti-tank operations deep behind Israeli lines. Under the command of Egyptian GHQ, commando forces, heli-lifted to pre-determined points, were to prevent Israeli tank formations from reaching the Bar Lev Line's second line of defence, and disrupt rear com-

munications and supply lines. The IAF shot down fourteen of the 33 Mi-8 helicopters ferrying the commandos, while mobile IDF units successfully dealt with those that managed to land intact.

Another setback was 3rd Mechanized Infantry Division's 130th Marine Brigade's attempt to cross the Little Bitter Lake in amphibious PT-76 tanks and BTR-50 and OT-62s. Their objective was to link up with commando forces in the Mitla and Gidi Passes. When many of the PT-76s were halfway across,

**Below:** A Centurion kicks up sand as it races to engage Egyptian T-62s which have just crossed the canal north of Botzer. (IDF Archives)

IDF armour opened fire. The lightly armoured PT-76s were no match for the accurate 105mm guns of the few Israeli Centurion and Patton tanks in position, and most were sunk. Those that managed to cross between BOTZER and LITUF raced for the Gidi Passes where they were eventually engaged by tanks from 401st Armoured Brigade heading for the front.

At 13.00 hours on 6 October, Albert was warned that an Egyptian artillery barrage on his positions was imminent. Albert immediately set operation SHOVACH YONIM in motion.

'SHOVACH YONIM' (Hebrew for pigeon-loft) was the code-name for the regular army's deployment plan in Sinai in event of war. It included all forces being placed on maximum alert, armoured forces to take up positions along the ramps, and for the MAOZIM to delay any Egyptian advances deeper into Sinai. The Egyptians defeated SHOVACH YONIM by simply crossing the canal at points not covered by the MAOZIM. Prior to the Egyptian blitz, and relying on his better instincts, Albert had ordered 401st Armoured Brigade to position itself near the front, ready itself for battle and defending the brigade from air attack (as a result, not one of Colonel Shomron's tanks was hit during the initial attack). On 5 October, Albert planned to move his entire division to the front, but was ordered not to do so by Gonen, 'so as not to provoke the Egyptians'. Albert, a soldier of supreme loyalty, refused to disobey his commander's orders. As reports flooded in of the crossing, Albert was heard mumbling to himself in his HQ. 'I warned them, but no one listened.' Albert tried to communicate with all the embattled Bar Lev positions, and spoke to the men calmly. When the division's young operations officer relayed orders to one of the MAOZIM in a frantic manner, Albert scolded him saying, 'We don't yell here.'

Albert's first priority was to rush his armoured brigades toward the line. Believing the main Egyptian thrust lay in the area of Tasa, 14th Armoured Brigade was ordered to the area and prepare to counter-attack. But when Albert learned that the situation was more threatening in the north, he ordered Amir's brigade there immediately. The situation was confusing at best, with no one at divisional HQ sure which routes were blocked by commando forces, and which ones were open. Meanwhile reports began to filter through from the positions. MATZMED reported a major breakthrough north of the Great Bitter Lake, while an Egyptian flag was raised upon MILANO ALEPH (the forward pillbox outpost of the MILANO complex). A fierce battle raged in the northern sector across from Port Said at positions ORKAL and LAHTZANIT. Requests for assistance were heard from ORKAL, with no response heard from LAHTZANIT. At 16.55 hours, the Egyptians constructed their first bridge across the canal north of PURKAN, across from Isma'iliya.

**THE EGYPTIAN CROSSING OF THE SUEZ CANAL**
**6 October 1973**

Lake Manzala

MEDITERRANEAN SEA

PORT SAID
PORT FUAD

ORKAL
BUDAPEST

LAHTZANIT

Suez Canal

DRORA

KETUBA

EGYPTIAN 2nd ARMY
16th, 2nd and 18th
Infantry Divisions
+ 14th, 24th and 15th
Armoured Brigades
+ 21st Armoured and
23rd Mechanized
Division

MILANO
MIFREKET

HIZAYON

ISMA'ILIYA

TASA

Khatmia Pass

PURKAN

EGYPT

MATZMED
LAKEKAN

XXXX
Great
Bitter Lake

ARTILLERY ROAD

LATERAL ROAD

130th Marine
Brigade in PT76s

BOTZER

Gidi Pass

EGYPTIAN 3rd ARMY
19th and 7th Infantry
Divisions + 22nd and
25th Armoured Brigades
+ 4th Armoured and 6th
Mechanized Divisions

LITUF

MAFZEAH

Mitla Pass

NISSAN

QUAY

Gulf of Suez

★ Israeli defensive position.

0  5  10  15  20  25  30  Kms
0  5    10    15    20  Miles

The Egyptian crossing was a much larger effort than had been predicted in IDF war games; as a result no immediate response ensued. Instead of the three armoured brigades intended to be deployed along the canal, only three tanks were in position. Colonel Reshef raced his 14th Armoured Brigade to the front, and was forced to divide his forces, sending them towards the ramps *ad hoc* in platoon and company strengths. On arrival at the ramps, the tank forces were decimated by the waiting commando anti-tank teams. At 19.35 hours 14th Armoured Brigade was ordered to reach PURKAN and destroy the Egyptian PMP bridge under construction. A battalion commanded by Lieutenant-Colonel Shlomoh Nitzani managed to position itself in an ideal firing position, and succeeded in destroying dozens of Egyptian APCs and tanks crossing the bridge. Although the force managed to damage the bridge severely, its section make-up enabled the Egyptians quickly to return them to operational use.

Hampering UGDAT ALBERT's holding effort was the lack of accurate front-line Intelligence.

Divisional Intelligence believed that the MAOZIM were successfully holding the line, and as a result their evacuation was not considered. When it became clear that most of the MAOZIM had fallen, and the remainder were surrounded, Albert ordered tank forces to relieve them, but anti-tank ambushes prohibited their approaching the besieged positions; especially LITUF, where 14th Armoured Brigade sustained heavy losses. As night fell, Albert ordered 460th Armoured Brigade to mount a counter-attack against the Egyptian bridgehead between LITUF and MAFZEAH. Just before dawn on 7 October, 460th Armoured Brigade mounted the first serious counter-attack in the south. The 460th Armoured Brigade's attack on Egyptian armour formations which had just crossed the canal proved a success. Firing at long ranges, Colonel Amir's M-60 Patton and Centurion tanks managed to destroy 67 T-62 and T-55 tanks without loss. Egyptian tank crews abandoned their vehicles in great haste, even before being hit by the Israeli 105mms! The closer 460th Armoured Brigade got to the canal, the

**Below:** An M-48 from an unidentified armoured battalion's SAYERET (marking on mudguard) heads towards an ambush position during the early morning of 7 October. (IDF Archives)

greater resistance it faced from commando anti-tank units who managed to destroy a large number of the force's tanks. At the same time, an infantry attack was mounted against Amir's left flank, from where the Egyptians had thrown up another bridge. The 460th Armoured Brigade was forced to retreat.

## UGDAT BREN

At 07.20 hours, the IAF mounted its first and only attack against the Egyptian bridges. IDF, General Staff decided to concentrate its air power against the more threatening situation developing with the Syrians up north. Albert, knowing that without adequate air-cover his forces could not counter-attack, ordered his tanks to disengage the enemy and fall back. The situation appeared hopeless, until 10.23 hours when Gonen informed Albert that help was on the way. Help came in the form of one, Major-General Avraham 'Bren' Adan, GOC, Armoured Corps, as he led an activated armoured division towards the front. UGDAT BREN was given responsibility for the northern sector of the front, stretching from Port Said south to Tasa; the 460th Armoured Brigade, fighting in the area, was transferred to Bren's command.

On 6 October at 06.00 hours Bren was summoned urgently to GHQ where he received word of impending war, and was ordered by Chief of Staff Elazar to take command of an armoured division (Brigadier-General Mordechai Tzipori received command of the Armoured Corps, although Bren was still in command of the corps' reservist mobilization process). Bren, who after thirty years of combat duty, first with the PAL'MACH, then the GIVA'ATI Infantry Brigade and finally with the Armoured Corps, was due to retire from the IDF in October 1973. He now prepared for his fifth war. At the same time, making its way to the front was Major-General (Res) Arik Sharon's reserve division. UGDAT ARIK was to be responsible for the central sector, and 14th Armoured Brigade was transferred to UGDAT SHARON. Gonen ordered Albert (now left with only Colonel Dan Shomron's 401st Armoured Brigade) to hold the southern sector at any cost

until relieved by the reservists. UGDAT ALBERT had only 96 operational tanks remaining along the Suez Canal. At 11.00 hours, Major-General Gonen ordered the evacuation of the MAOZIM.

At midday on 7 October, the Egyptian 7th Infantry Division and 25th Independent Armoured Brigade had completed its crossing south of the Great Bitter Lake. An Israeli counter-attack was already under way, even as the Egyptians consolidated their positions and proceeded to widen their bridgeheads to 5–6 miles in depth. At a command conference held in Sinai, Chief of Staff Lieutenant-General Elazar, Majors-General Gonen, Mandler, and Adan (Sharon was conspicuously absent) planned the counter-attack. Gonen suggested seizing the existing Egyptian bridges and using them for an Israeli crossing, but both Albert and Adan knew the exhausted and depleted forces at their disposal could not achieve such a major operation. UGDAT ALBERT had been fighting non-stop for 36 hours and Bren's tanks had driven all night, the entire length of Sinai on their tracks, in their race to the front. Elazar concluded that immediate action was necessary in order to control the rapidly deteriorating military situation. He ordered UGDAT BREN to break into the Egyptian Second Army's southern flank, attacking along the north-south axis from El-Qantara to the Great Bitter Lake, with UGDAT SHARON held in mobile reserve; in the event, UGDAT BREN achieved a breakthrough. UGDAT SHARON was to proceed southwards attacking the Third Army.

Hours before the attack, only two of UGDAT BREN's armoured brigades were available for immediate offensive deployment; the 460th (with only 51 tanks remaining) and the 217th Armoured Brigade (equipped with Centurions) commanded by Colonel Natan 'Natke' Nir. As a battalion commander during the Six Day War, he had been so gravely wounded that he had to be hoisted into his command tank. Although undergoing more than twenty operations between 1967 and 1973, Nir refused to retire from active duty, and the presence of this indestructible fighter greatly improved morale. A third brigade, the 500th Armoured Brigade, commanded by Colonel Arieh Keren, was still at its staging-post in northern Sinai, and would have to join the attack in progress. UGDAT BREN was hampered at the outset by having to dispatch its recon force to hunt down commando anti-tank teams. Without his SAYERET

UGDATIT to lead the way, Major-General Adan was forced to inch his way forward without reliable advanced field Intelligence. Nevertheless, at 08.00 hours on 8 October, the counterattack began. The 460th Armoured Brigade attempted to reach the water line positions opposite El Firdan, while 500th Armoured Brigade attempted to relieve pressure on MATZMED on the northernmost bank of the Great Bitter Lake. The attack went poorly for the Israelis as IAF aircraft mistakenly attacked a lead column of Colonel Nir's tanks, while effective jamming of Bren's radio frequency caused him to lose contact with most of his division for more than two hours. Bren's advance faced minimal opposition as it bypassed major points of Egyptian armour concentration. This led to unjustified optimism at Southern Command HQ, and Gonen ordered UGDAT SHARON to proceed in attacking the Third Army.

With UGDAT SHARON no longer protecting his left flank, Bren's armour forces came under intense artillery and anti-tank fire. Its losses were heavy, with RPG and Sagger fire taking its murderous toll. UGDAT BREN lacked the infantry support needed to defeat the anti-tank teams. Sensing victory, the Egyptians mounted their own counter-attack, throwing the 2nd and 16th Infantry Divisions (together with the 117th and 3rd Mechanized Infantry and the 14th and 24th Tank Brigades) against Bren's already battered forces. This covered the 21st Armoured and 23rd Mechanized Division's non-stop crossing of the canal. As darkness fell Bren withdrew, suffering heavy casualties with 73 of his 175 tanks destroyed. The failed counter-attack did however buy invaluable time for reservist units to reach the front, and for the military options to be reconsidered.

## TURNING-POINT IN THE DESERT – THE BATTLE OF 14 OCTOBER

In the evening of 8 October, the three divisional commanders together with Chief of Staff Elazar and Defence Minister Dayan met at the underground command complex at Um-Khusheiba. The atmosphere was tense; the failure of the counter-attack had taken its psychological and physical toll of the generals who had been spoiled by their past lightning victories. All the commanders appeared exhausted and unkept except Albert who, characteristically, arrived clean shaven, in a pressed uniform and with boots shining brilliantly. Gonen concluded that Southern Command could not withstand another such day, with so little progress and so many casualties, as UGDAT BREN had endured. He ordered his commanders to refrain from further counterattacks, and to await the reservists before undertaking a major move. Sharon was outraged by this appeasing attitude, but Albert, although disagreeing with Gonen, supported his commander's orders.

At 22.00 hours on 8 October, UGDAT ALBERT's Intelligence officer reported a major breakthrough by the Egyptian 18th Infantry Division (supported by an independent armoured brigade) in the area of El-Qantara. At the same time, 2nd Armoured Division together with organic infantry forces strengthened their positions near Isma'ilya, while 16th Infantry Division with armoured elements succeeded in breaking out of their beachhead between Lake Timsah and the Great Bitter Lake. There were more than 400 Egyptian tanks in the area of LITUF, and the Third Army's 7th and 19th Infantry Divisions, together with two armoured brigades, pushed deeper into Sinai.

By 9 October Egyptian consolidation of the east bank was such that the Israelis had no choice but to avoid major contact. Albert took command of Colonel Avraham Bar-Am's HAREL Armoured Brigade and ordered the tankers to refrain from engaging the enemy *unless* they could be forced into a long-range mobile action. The Egyptians, still on the offensive, resumed their efforts to seize the second-line strongholds of KFAR and MEZACH. 401st Armoured Brigade recon battalion engaged an Egyptian force of two brigades, destroying more than 32 tanks and vehicles. But Shomron knew he couldn't relieve the pressure on KFAR, and was forced to fall back. The position fell later that day, MAFTZEAH fell the day after, but MEZACH held out. At 09.30 hours the Egyptians attacked with such strength along the line, that Albert gave orders for all female soldiers to be evacuated from rear bases, and for these bases to prepare their defences. The Centurion tanks from HATIVAT

HAREL engaged the numerically superior Egyptian armour which advanced head-on into the brigade's defensive position, destroying more than fifty T-55s. The Egyptians retreated quickly without stopping to pick up their wounded. The Sinai front had, in effect, stabilized, with Egyptian forces achieving no more territorial advances throughout the remainder of the war. Each day Egyptian forces mounted attacks on the Israeli line. Familiarity with the terrain and the punctuality of the attacks led to an increasing degree of self-confidence among the Israeli tankers, who were able to hold off Egyptian offensive attempts with minimal casualties. Israeli forces now began to take control of the battlefield, reservists were reaching the front in substantial numbers, and the tide seemed to have turned in the IDF's favour.

As Israeli forces increased in size, planning for the crossing of the canal commenced. An IDF crossing of the canal into Egypt proper had been a fundamental facet of IDF military strategy since 1968. Inflatable boats and pre-constructed bridges were stored in Engineer Corps supply bases throughout Sinai, and specially designed roads were in place so that the bridges could be towed towards the waterline. By 10 October, Southern Command had two options: to seize existing Egyptian bridges and cross immediately, or decisively to defeat a large Egyptian force, and then counter-attack across the canal. Lieutenant-General (Res) Haim Bar-Lev, who had been sent to Southern Command as Prime Minister Meir's personal representative at the front (replacing Gonen in whom confidence had fallen to a low level), opted for the latter plan and agreed with Gonen's assessment that the crossing should take place at Deversoir. Deversoir's location was ideal for the crossing since it was one of the eastern points on the west bank waterline for IDF forces to reach without a major battle; its southern flank was protected by the Great Bitter Lake, and the area across the canal at this point was more conducive to mobile armoured advances by the IDF. Also, it was a soft underbelly, the boundary line between the Egyptian Second and Third Armies. At midnight on 10 October, the bridge was ordered out of storage, and was made ready to move out at a minute's notice. The exact timing of the crossing was still undecided, although it was agreed that it could take place only *after* a serious dent in the Egyptian forces had been made.

Also on 10 October a badly needed fourth armoured brigade, KOACH GONEN (Force Gonen), was reaching UGDAT BREN. Commanded by Colonel Yoel Gonen (Southern Command commander's younger brother), KOACH GONEN was equipped with Egyptian and Syrian T-55s captured during the Six Day War and re-armed with 105mm guns. KOACH GONEN's reconnaissance companies (equipped with captured mobile BTRs and PT-76s) was considered one of the finest armoured SAYEROT in the IDF and had partaken in numerous cross-canal commando raids during the War of Attrition. The arrival of KOACH GONEN, a seasoned and capable force, helped create strategic reserves for UGDAT BREN, the most exposed of Southern Command's three divisions.

According to Soviet doctrine, the Egyptians should have mounted a major armour offensive on 11/12 October. Elazar, with all divisional commanders in agreement (with the exception of Sharon who argued vehemently that a crossing could succeed immediately), decided to wait, and defeat the expected major Egyptian push. UGDAT BREN was removed from the line to prepare for the crossing, while UGDOT SHARON and ALBERT were placed in defensive positions. Major disagreements regarding tactics on the Sinai front were dividing the Egyptian camp. Shazli favoured any Egyptian offensive to move up the Mediterranean coast towards El-Arish, but he was against any further push until the SAM umbrella crossed the canal to protect his forces. The SAM umbrella would not cross to the east bank of the canal until the Egyptians decisively defeated the IDF armour presence. Egyptian Minister of War, General Ismail, also favoured waiting for the front to stabilize until moving the SAMs across the canal, but on 11 October the Syrians sent Ismail an urgent plea for help to reduce IDF pressure on the Golan. Ismail, also Joint Arab Armies Commander-in-Chief, felt a responsibility for Arab military solidarity (so painfully missing during past conflicts with Israel) and decided to authorize a limited armoured offensive for 13 October (which was put back to the 14th).

On the night of 12/13 October, the Second Army's 21st Armoured Division and a mechanized brigade from the 23rd Mechanized Division crossed the canal, while a major force from the Third Army's 4th Armoured Division and

**Right:** MAG'ACHIM of HATIVAT SHOMRON prepare for battle, 10 October 1973, at a forward ordnance base near the canal. (IDF Archives)

**Far right:** A Centurion from Colonel Nir's 217th Armoured Brigade joins in an artillery barrage on Egyptian commando concentrations, 12 October 1973. (IDF Archives)

**Right:** MAG'ACHIM from 14th Armoured Brigade race to counter-attack Egyptian armour concentrations near the water line. (IDF Archives)

the 6th Mechanized Division crossed over in their sector. SAM batteries were also moved to the east bank. On 13 October, Second and Third Armies launched probing attacks along the entire length of the front with a view to capturing the three strategic passes, Khatmia, Gidi and Mitla, and then pushing on towards the command centres of Tasa and Refidim. In response to the Egyptian moves, Gonen deployed his forces along the entire length of the front. UGDOT ALBERT and SHARON would beat off the Egyptian attack, with UGDAT BREN (busily preparing for the crossing) held as strategic reserve. On the 13th, the penultimate uncaptured MAOZ of Quay, opposite Port Tewfik, fell. The defenders had fought gallantly, but with many wounded and all medical supplies exhausted, its commander, Lieutenant Shlomoh Ardinest, had no option but to surrender. He ordered his men to wash and change into clean uniforms, and march in parade formation into captivity. Armed with white flag and the Torah, Lieutenant Ardinest surrendered to Egyptian soldiers looking on in awe.

On 13 October at 08.00 hours, UGDAT ALBERT was involved in holding Egyptian attempts to take MEZACH. While Gonen was on the radio discussing the battle with Albert, the radio went silent. Gonen knew immediately that Albert was dead. Accurately ranged by an infantry anti-tank team, Albert's M113 command post had been hit by a Sagger missile. His death was a tremendous blow for Southern Command. Albert was considered to be one of the finest armoured officers in the IDF's short but battle-scarred history. Born in Lintz, Austria in 1929, Albert was one of the few senior IDF officers to have personally experienced the Nazi horror. He managed to escape from Austria in 1940, and at the age of 16, he joined the GAD'NA (Hebrew acronym for 'Youth Battalions'), and with the outbreak of the 1948 War of Independence, joined the IDF. He eventually found his way to GIVA'ATI Brigade's élite 54th Battalion, and then to SHU'ALEI SHIMSHON (Southern Command's recon battalion) where he reached the rank of First Lieutenant. In 1950 Albert left the IDF, but returned shortly afterwards, asking to serve

in the fledgling Armoured Corps. Albert loved tanks, HEYL SHIRION, and the desert. His claim to military fame was as commander of the armoured brigade which stormed up the Golan Heights and captured Kuneitra during the 1967 War. Albert was one of the few line commanders who knew that war was imminent in October 1973, and tried his best to ready his division for the coming conflict that his superiors refused to acknowledge. Gonen flew to Sharon's advanced headquarters with news of Albert's death; and turned command of his division over to Major-General Kalman Magen, who was commanding forces in the northernmost sector in Sinai.

At 06.00 hours on 14 October, the Egyptians launched their long-awaited attack. An intensive 30-minute artillery barrage preceded the armoured forces' major push. At 06.30 hours, six armoured attacks (in independent columns of a brigade each) thrust eastwards from Egyptian positions. Second Army's attack (half of the entire offensive push that day) was commanded by General Mamoun from his HQ in Isma'ilya. In Second Army's northern sector, the 18th Infantry Division, with an armoured brigade equipped with T-62s, advanced from El-Qantara in an endeavour to capture ROMANI. From Isma'iliya, 21st Armoured Division, together with a tank brigade from 23rd Mechanized Division, broke out along the central sector towards Tasa and the Khatmia Pass. Under the command of General Wassel, Third Army's northernmost push was made by the 7th Infantry Division in its drive towards the Gidi Pass and Southern Command's advance headquarters at Um-Khusheiba. The 19th Division struck southwards towards the Mitla Pass, while armoured elements from the division headed towards the Sudr Pass (near the major oil installations) just south of Mitla.

The Egyptians deployed well over 1,200 tanks, while the Israelis had more than 750 tanks in their positions. Thus began the largest tank battle since the Second World War, and the second largest in military history after the battle for Kursk. In the northernmost sector, the Egyptians pressed hard against the thinly spread forces of UGDAT SASSON (the division commanded by Brigadier General Sassoon, who had taken over the forces under Major-General Kalman Magen's command on the northernmost sector of the Sinai front). UGDAT BREN, which had been taken off the line to prepare for the crossing, was called in and took immediate control of the area, repelling the Egyptian advance and destroying more than 55 T-62s. The Second Army's central advance against UGDAT ARIK fared no better. The division's Patton tanks made the most of the terrain with which they had so familiarized themselves during numerous training exercises and engaged the Egyptians at long range. After fifty minutes of fighting, the Egyptians withdrew, leaving sixty smouldering T-55s on the battlefield. The only Egyptian success at the outset of the battle was against UGDAT SASSON's thinly held defences. As a result of the attrition on this division from 6 October until the 14th, the Egyptians succeeded in making initial gains, although these 'achievements' were retaken by 17.00 hours. The 7th and 19th Divisions failed to reach their primary objective, the Lateral Road, and by 19.00 hours, they were in retreat leaving 62 tanks behind. The greatest Egyptian losses of the day (preceded by their greatest initial success) came in the southernmost sector with the attack towards Sudr where they succeeded in breaking through to a depth of fourteen miles. A combined paratroop/armour 'last stand' unit managed to halt the Egyptian advance, but by dusk it was forced to withdraw leaving nearly 100 tanks destroyed on the battlefield.

Psychologically the Israeli troops were 'up' for the battle. Now confident in their numbers, and having got over the initial trauma of the Egyptian blitz, the men of Southern Command were prepared for any contingency. The threat of infantry anti-tank teams was diminished by attaching an APC (an M113 or an M3 Half-track) to every two tanks, usually positioned at 45° on each flank. Tanks (mainly from brigade or battalion recon units) left their defensive positions and exposed themselves to infantry anti-tank fire. While each tank changed its position to avoid fire, the APC raced towards the anti-tank teams who had exposed their concealed positions. This deployment plan succeeded in decreasing the threat of infantry anti-tank missile teams, and allowed IDF armour to concentrate only on advancing enemy armour. The tell-tale signs of hundreds of guide wires littered the battlefield.

In training exercises, the IDF prides itself on the long-range accuracy of its tank gunners, and on 14 October even the most modest gunnery instructor would have been proud of his pupils.

**Above:** A relaxed moment on the Lateral Road. A PT-76 from KOACH GONEN passes a MAG'ACH undergoing field repairs. (IDF Archives)

**Left:** A reconnaissance OT-62 in IDF service. Note battalion flag, and rear area painted white for night time station keeping. (IDF Archives)

**Above:** Modified and up-gunned Shermans prepare to deploy for the major tank battle of 14 October 1973. Operational reports from the battle indicate that the 'obsolete' Shermans did quite well in the desert. (IDF Archives)

**Right:** An M3 Halftrack TA'GAD (battalion medevac station) of 14th Armoured Brigade's 1st Battalion, searches for wounded after the fierce battle of 9 October. (IDF Archives)

Brigade commanders in all the UGDOT on the line allowed the Egyptians to advance to within about 500 yards and then ordered the guns to open fire. The sheer numerical weight of the Egyptian attack allowed many tanks to break through the 'fire-line', and these tanks were quickly taken care of by the Centurions, Pattons and Shermans positioned in V formation. Firing from hull-down positions, they made the most of the desert terrain for camouflage. The tanks fought the battle divided in company strengths; after firing a volley, they retreated to their defensive EMDOT (firing positions). This not only confused Egyptian artillery spotters, but also kept the battle constantly mobile, tactics at which the Israeli tankers excelled. UGDAT SHARON allowed Egyptian armour to enter a planned killing ground and when they were trapped the Pattons charged in 'Wild West style' shooting from long range. At many points the Egyptians advanced beyond their SAM umbrella, and for the first time since the outbreak of war on the Sinai front, the IAF was able to enter the fray unmolested, taking a heavy toll of the Egyptian armour and mechanized formations.

The Egyptians too had been eager for the battle, but by mid-evening, General Ismail realized that his forces had not achieved a major breakthrough; in fact they had not advanced at all. In his heart he knew that placing his forces beyond the SAM protection was a tactical mistake, and fearing *major* losses he recalled all forces back to their starting-point. Egyptian losses for the day were staggering. In less than twelve hours of battle, they left in the desert 264 tanks destroyed and suffered more than 1,000 casualties. Only six Israeli tanks were lost that day. Southern Command, rejoicing in the major victory, prepared to cross the canal into Africa.

## OPERATION 'STOUT-HEARTED', 'CHINESE FARM' AND SUEZ

MIVTZA ABIREY LEV (Operation 'Stout-Hearted'), the IDF's pre-war plan for crossing the Canal, was devised by Major-General Sharon during his tenure as GOC, Southern Command. It called for a crossing by two

divisions, the establishment of a bridgehead or the west bank, with forces taking control of the area between the Sweet Water Canal (which brings the Nile's waters to Isma'iliya) and Jebel Ubed, Jebel Ataka, and Suez. Armoured columns were to destroy Egyptian forces in the area, and then outflank and eventually surround and cut off Egyptian forces on the east bank. Southern Command determined that the crossing would take place in the area of MATZMED, which is close to the northern shores of the Great Bitter Lake. At MATZMED Sharon authorized the laying down of a hard brick surface area, 700 yards by 500 yards, with surrounding protective sand barriers. The 'yard' as it became known was the designated spot from where the crossing of the Canal would take place. MATZMED was also central to essential military objectives for IDF forces; north-west of MATZMED were four paths across the Isma'iliya Canal whose capture could enable the isolation of Egyptian forces in the northern sector. South-west of MATZMED tower the Genefa Hills which dominated the routes to Cairo and Suez.

On 14 October at 22.40 hours, ABIREV LEV was formally presented at a Southern Command staff meeting. According to the plan, UGDAT ARIK would advance towards MATZMED, set the pre-constructed bridge in position, and cross at Deversoir, securing both banks of the Canal. Once the area was secured, UGDAT BREN would break out southwards and westwards in the Genefa Hills, eventually reaching, isolating and capturing Suez. UGDAT SASSON would then assume control of the east bank, allowing UGDAT ARIK to cross over and head south. The bridges were to be assembled during the first night of the operation, the armoured breakout achieved by the second night, and the capture of Suez in the following days. Leading the crossing of the Canal was the PLUGAT SIYUR HATIVATIT (brigade reconnaissance company) from the 247th Reserve Paratroop Brigade commanded by Colonel Dani Matt. UGDAT ARIK's three armoured brigades; Colonel Reshef's 14th Armoured Brigade, Colonel Tuvia Raviv's 600th Armoured Brigade, and Colonel Haim Erez's HATIVAT HAIM had a total strength of 274 tanks. The 600th Armoured Brigade would commence the operation with a diversionary attack eastwards.

With the diversionary attack under way, 14th Armoured Brigade's four tank battalions (including one from 600th Armoured Brigade) and three mechanized infantry battalions (including recon companies) would break through the boundary line between Second and Third Armies and proceed on to the LEXICON route undetected. The Brigade would then swing northwards, attempting to capture the 'Chinese Farm'. The 14th Armoured Brigade would also attempt to open the TIRTUR and AKAVISH routes west to east. Once the routes were open and free of enemy forces, the two 'crossing' brigades would advance towards the

Canal together with the crossing equipment. Colonel Matt's paratroopers would advance up AKAVISH (together with tank ferries and rubber craft brought up by combat engineers) with their M3 Halftracks, while HATIVAT HAIM would advance up TIRTUR towing the bridge. Matt's paratroopers were to have sixty half-tracks and sixty inflatable boats, but by 10.00 hours on 15 October, none of these had arrived. Bren, feared major holdups along the route towards the bridges, and decided against moving his forces along AKAVISH. He also organized special 'refuelling units' on M113s which travelled with the tank columns on the roads though impassable sand dunes.

At 17.00 hours (until 21.00 hours) on 15 October, the crossing operation went into high gear. While the 600th Armoured Brigade 'occupied' the Egyptians with diversionary attacks, 14th Armoured Brigade broke out from LEXICON and at 23.30 hours Colonel Matt's paratroopers received the order to cross with its protecting tanks from Colonel Erez's brigade. The force moved into the 'yard' and prepared for the crossing. Two battalions of paratroopers led by the brigade's recon company began the crossing at 01.25 on 16 October, after a massive IDF artillery bombardment on the west bank; which fell on mostly silent ground as no enemy forces were reported in the area. Minutes later Colonel Matt radioed to Sharon's HQ 'Acapulco . . . Acapulco . . .', the code-word indicating his forces had reached the west bank safely. Until 03.00 hours, Matt consolidated his position on the west bank, opening an area 1,000 yards wide by 225 yards deep. Matt reinforced his bridgehead with an advanced brigade HQ, and a further two battalions. The only encountered resistance was from some artillery fire, but the shells were few and far between. By dawn the brigade had fanned out, with 750 paratroopers in three battalions (416th, 564th and 565th) equipped with short-range anti-tank weapons (mainly captured RPGs, rifle grenades, and LAW 66m rockets). The area was secure enough for the first tanks of HATIVAT HAIM to cross on rafts by 06.43 hours. Besides protecting Matt's paratroopers, HATIVAT HAIM was also entrusted with the vital mission of destroying SAM bases on the west bank, which would enable the IAF to fly ground support missions.

Meanwhile, the battle raged north of MATZMED with the roads clogged with armour

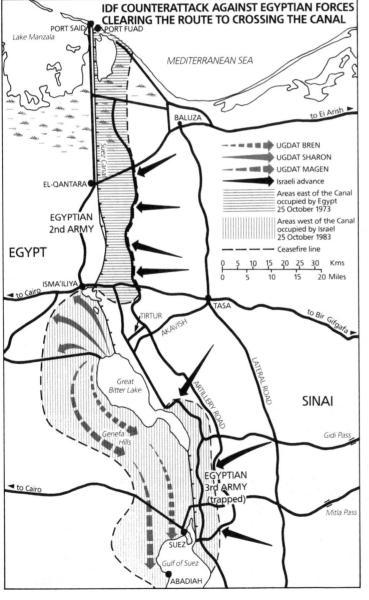

and APCs. The opening and securing of TIRTUR was essential for the success of the operation, for unless the lines of communications could be kept open, the entire operation was in danger. Defence Minister Dayan, worried with the developing situation on the clogged routes, suggested that Matt's paratroopers return from the west bank. Gonen disagreed, arguing that since the effort to cross was in progress, the operation should continue as planned. A major debate was also developing between Sharon and Southern Command. Sharon urged that the bridgehead on the west bank be exploited immediately, while the rest of

the command intended to await the opening of the routes, and the arrival of UGDAT BREN. Incensed, Sharon shouted 'this is not a damn raid across the water, it is a major undertaking' and urged that UGDAT BREN follow *his* division's crossing of the Canal on ferries. Bar-Lev disagreed and turned down Sharon, insisting that a major operation of this nature could not rely on the vulnerable ferries. The push to open the routes continued, but with little initial success.

At 03.00 hours, Colonel Reshef, commanding Major Yoav Brum's G'DUD SIYUR, attacked the AKAVISH-TIRTUR crossroads. The 14th

**Below:** 'Chinese Farm' during the battle. Note bullet-holes 'decorating' building in background. (IDF Archives)

Armoured Brigade had entered the 'rear door' of the Egyptian 16th Infantry Division's logistical nerve centre, and thousands of troops were milling about in the area. In addition, 21st Armoured Division had set up camp in the area following its decimation in the battle of 14 October. The G'DUD SIYUR suddenly found itself in the centre of hundreds of tanks, APCs, artillery pieces and soldiers, all of whom opened fire on Reshef's small tank force. In the opening moments of the mêlée Reshef lost eleven tanks including Major Brum's which received a direct RPG hit between the hull and turret, killing the young officer. A platoon from the division's

recon force commanded by Lieutenant Rafi Bar-Lev attempted to assist Reshef to extricate his forces, but Bar-Lev (nephew of the former Chief of Staff) was killed in the cross-fire. Among the many who fell that evening was Captain Gideon Gila'adi, a company commander in 14th Armoured Brigade. Gila'adi had been ordered to take TIRTUR, but at the TIRTUR-LEXICON crossroads his troops ran into an Egyptian anti-tank ambush. Gila'adi's tank was immediately set ablaze, and he ran to assume command from another vehicle. He led the company in attacking the crossroads time and time again, until he had only two operational tanks left. Undaunted, Captain Gila'adi attacked TIRTUR with his remaining two tanks, and was killed. Gila'adi was awarded the Order of Bravery posthumously. What makes Gila'adi's experience so tragic, and yet typical of IDF officers, is that he had been a paratroop officer until 1967 (when his brother was killed as a 7th Brigade company commander). Vowing that he would one day command his brother's unit, Gila'adi transferred to the Armoured Corps and eventually achieved his goal only months before the war.

That night's battle was one of the bloodiest of the war, fought at ranges varying between 500 yards and hand-to-hand. Wounded were unable to be evacuated, and Reshef's lead tank had to be used as the brigade's field dressing station. During the night, 14th Armoured Brigade lost sixty tanks, and was left with only forty operational vehicles. In addition, 121 men were killed (including 43 officers) during the 12-hour battle.

Sharon urged Colonel Reshef to exert maximum pressure to open the TIRTUR route. With Egyptian resistance so heavy and determined, this task was too much for the already exhausted tankers; they were reduced to advancing piecemeal, fighting in platoon, company, and even squad strengths, without substantial military coherence. At 04.25 hours HATIVAT HAIM's recon battalion (heading north-east) attempted to open the TIRTUR route. This attack sustained heavy casualties from a highly effective anti-tank missile screen in place near the 'Chinese Farm'. Two tanks were destroyed and the battalion was forced to withdraw (taking with them the wounded from the previous night's battle). An hour later Reshef returned, this time attempting to open TIRTUR from the east. A total of 22 tanks from 600th

**Right:** A pre-battle briefing atop a Centurion from 460th Armoured Brigade. (IDF Archives)

**Right:** A pre-battle briefing atop a Centurion from 460th Armoured Brigade. (IDF Archives)

Armoured Brigade led the attack, which failed after four of their tanks went up in flames immediately. Colonel Reshef regrouped and attacked the LEXICON-TIRTUR crossroads with thirteen tanks from his G'DUD SIYUR together with eighteen remaining tanks from 600th Armoured Brigade's battalion on loan to him, and two companies of recon paratroopers on M3 Halftracks. Egyptian dug-in tank and infantry concentrations were strong in the area, and a close-range battle erupted. The Egyptians too had been fighting almost non-stop for twelve hours, and their exhaustion was now apparent. The cramped and confined conditions inside their Soviet-built tanks also began to take its toll, and the Egyptian tank formation withdrew. Fatigued, Colonel Reshef radioed Sharon at 08.40 hours that the crossroads were in IDF hands.

From the outset of the operation, Brigadier-General Jackie Even (deputy commander of UGDAT ARIK) commanded the operation to 'open' AKAVISH. AKAVISH was the only route running directly from Tasa towards MATZMED, and was the road on which the pre-constructed bridges were to be towed. Hundreds of tanks (including those towing the bridges), refuelling trucks and APCs were held up for sixteen miles by enormous traffic jams which plagued this

15-foot wide road. Any vehicle that attempted to by-pass along the surrounding dunes sank into the deep banks of sand. HATIVAT HAIM, together with three companies of combat engineers, were frantic in their efforts to get the bridging equipment towards the crossing-point. A second tank force secured the arrival of French-built 'Gilowa' raft bridges towards MATZMED while a third tank force (in company strength) raced ahead of these columns, securing their path.

At midnight, Lieutenant-General Bar-Lev and Sharon decided to race the pontoon bridges towards the 'yard' in order to rush as much armour as possible to Matt's para-troopers. Eighteen Gilowas were dispatched with two lead companies from HATIVAT HAIM; they reached the Canal at 04.00 hours on 16 October. The large pre-constructed bridge was still held up on AKAVISH. Towing the 400-ton bridge caused numerous accompanying tanks to break down; and at 05.00 hours the bridge itself suffered mechanical failure. With every passing moment Sharon feared that the Egyptians would discover what he was up to. He ordered HATIVAT HAIM's 2nd Battalion to get to MATZMED and to cross the Canal.

At 08.47 hours, Colonel Haim Erez stood upright in his M-60 tank as his lead battalion (with a battalion from Colonel Matt's para-troopers) advanced along the AKAVISH route. The column came under murderous small-arms and anti-tank fire, and four tanks were immediately set ablaze. Small-arms fire had damaged his radio, so under heavy fire Erez raced towards the rear to order his exposed para-troopers to take cover. Realizing that AKAVISH was blocked, Erez ordered his unit to outflank the blocking enemy force, now reinforced with a T-62 battalion. In the meantime, efforts were under way at the 'yard', where the Gilowas began to ferry tank forces across the Canal. Once across, Colonel Matt integrated his para-troops with the newly arrived tank companies, and organized them at the Dawad Suar airfield. These units were then sent to attack Egyptian forces in the area, who were shocked to find IDF forces in 'Africa'. Matt also dispatched a recon company to block all routes to and from the Sweet Water Canal.

When Colonel Erez finally managed to reach the 'yard', Sharon immediately ordered him to cross and destroy Egyptian SAM bases on the west bank. Once across, Colonel Erez took 22 tanks and seven APCs (leaving seven Pattons behind to protect the bridgehead) and advanced fourteen miles south of the Canal, destroying four SAM bases, ten tanks, and 25 Egyptian BTRs in the process. At 16.00 hours his forces returned to the bridgehead to take on fuel and ammunition, and evacuate the wounded. Colonel Reshef's efforts to break open the TIRTUR route on the morning of 16 October, and Colonel Erez's raid on the west bank allowed UGDAT ARIK to complete its primary objectives at ABIREY LEV, but a large part of UGDAT ARIK had been eroded by the previous day's heavy fighting. With part of the division on the west bank, and another part driving a wedge in the enemy's rear, the division had ceased to be an effective fighting force. In the east, TIRTUR and AKAVISH (where Sharon's deputy, Brigadier Even, and the bridging equipment were held up) were blocked. The only routes connecting the two forces on opposite sides of the Canal were sand routes, not conducive to mobility.

**Below:** A MAG'ACH from 460th Armoured Brigade tows a 'Gilowa' towards the 'Yard'. (IDF Archives)

According to the plan, Israel forces were to secure both banks of the bridgehead, while both TIRTUT and AKAVISH would be open, allowing the bridges to reach the 'yard'. In fact, the Israelis had only one narrow bridgehead, with all paths to the crossing-points blocked. UGDAT ARIK's strength was too depleted to be able to carry out its mission. There was an immediate danger that an Egyptian counter-attack would succeed in cutting off Colonel Matt's bridgehead. Southern Command concluded that until a large bridgehead had been established over the Canal, no more tanks would cross. Sharon vehemently protested this, insisting that the operation must proceed un-hindered. Lieutenant-General Elazar replied that it was 'dangerous' to move such a sub-stantial force across on only three Gilowas, whose endurance under fire was minimal. Bar-Lev issued an order to maintain the *status quo* and keep a low profile on the west bank, while major IDF efforts would be concentrated to open the routes, and proceed towards MATZMED. Only after Sharon could secure both sides of the bridgehead, would UGDAT BREN cross the bridges.

Throughout the night of 16 October, UGDAT BREN readied itself for the crossing, while Bren visited the damaged bridge, which combat engineers were frantically repairing. He urged Lieutenant-Colonel Haim Razon (one of the senior Armour Corps ordnance officers, who specialized in the rescue of heavy vehicles in the most difficult of conditions; usually under intense fire) to restore the bridge to operational status as soon as possible. In the meantime, Brigadier-General (Res) Uri Ben-Ari (who seventeen years earlier had led 7th Armoured Brigade to victory in these very same sands) arrived by helicopter, urging Bren to make his deputy, Brigadier-General Tamari respon-sible for the bridges and pontoons getting to the 'yard'. Tamari eventually succeeded in making room for twelve Gilowas to reach the Canal. Close to 12.00 hours on the 16th, Bren's command staff was instructed by Southern Command that UGDAT ARIK would seize the 'Chinese Farm', while UGDAT BREN opened up TIRTUR and AKAVISH.

Colonel Nir's 217th Armoured Brigade attacked along TIRTUR and AKAVISH, but was stopped and forced to withdraw as hundreds of

**Right:** 'Chinese Farm', an agricultural settlement in Sinai before the war. (IDF Archives)

Sagger missiles were fired from the 'Chinese Farm'. Bren ordered him to wait in the surrounding dunes, while the enemy left the concealed positions and entered the killing ground. Bren then ordered Colonel Amir's 460th Armoured Brigade to ready itself. The Egyptians refused the bait; instead they tried to lure the Israelis into the 'Chinese Farm' and a killing ground of their own. In early evening, Bren advised Southern Command that it would be safest to hold off until night and then clean out the 'Chinese Farm' using 35th Paratroop Brigade (the IDF's conscript paratroop brigade) commanded by Colonel Uzi Yairi. The Egyptians had not correctly appreciated Israeli intentions. They thought it was a limited crossing of the Canal, whose aims were psychological. As a result, the Egyptians decided to concentrate on destroying the IDF wedge on the east bank.

The 35th Brigade had been spread out in the Abu-Rods area near the Gulf of Suez, where they were engaging Egyptian commando forces. Colonel Yairi's helicopter did not land at Bren's war room until 22.00 hours. Time was of the essence, and since so many idle hours had been lost. Yairi threw his forces into battle without a proper briefing. The Egyptians had fortified the 'Chinese Farm', and Yairi's forces immediately suffered numerous casualties in bitter hand-to-hand fighting. Not only were the paratroopers unable to destroy the Egyptian forces in the area, but they found themselves pinned down under murderous small-arms and missile fire. The battle did manage to preoccupy the Egyptians so as to allow the pontoons and bridges to be brought up towards the water-line, and at 06.30 hours on the 17th, the first bridge was laid across the Canal. (Lieutenant-Colonel Yairi was killed two years later leading a rescue-assault on the Tel Aviv beachfront Savoy Hotel, held by seaborne Black September terrorists.)

At 08.00 hours, the Egyptians began to attack the IDF wedge in MATZMED's vicinity; and a major armour battle was under way at the 'Chinese Farm'. Colonel Reshef, whose brigade was regrouping at LAKEKAN on the shores of the Great Bitter Lake, radioed that what seemed to be an approaching armour force of substantial size was heading straight for 217th Armoured Brigade's line. Bren ordered aerial

**Right:** A command reconnaissance OT-62 prepares to cross the Canal. Although the Egyptian knew that the IDF had captured many such vehicles in 1967, they still confused Egyptian tankers in battle. (IDF Archives)

reconnaissance, and an RF-4E was airborne in minutes. The RF-4E's pilot confirmed that a column of approximately 100 T-62s was headed towards UGDAT BREN's line. It was the 25th Tank Brigade. Bren immediately ordered Colonel Nir to move his brigade into ambush to destroy the advancing enemy armour. The 500th Armoured Brigade was dispatched to assist Colonel Nir, and at 14.45 hours the battle began. Unsuspecting, the 25th Tank Brigade continued its advance with 96 T-62s, and dozens of APCs, artillery pieces, and supply vehicles. The 217th Armoured Brigade opened fire at long range, destroying dozens of enemy tanks. At 15.00 hours, as the Egyptians closed in, Nir's tanks moved out from their concealed positions and attacked them from both flanks. Dozens more Egyptian tanks were set ablaze, and Nir's tanks closed the range. The 25th Brigade was trapped in open low ground, totally surrounded. After engaging the 217th Armoured Brigade for thirty minutes, 25th Brigade was hemmed in as 500th Armoured Brigade moved in from the Gidi road. UGDAT SASSON assisted the 500th Armoured Brigade's effort with concentrated artillery support. The area became an immense killing ground for 25th Brigade, as tank after tank was picked off. Many tanks tried to flee, but were chased by Colonel Keren's tanks. In fact the only Israeli tank losses of the day were four tanks which blew up on mines placed by IDF during the War of Attrition. By 17.00 hours, 25th Brigade had ceased to exist. Eighty-six T-62s had been destroyed, the remaining ten tanks escaping into the BOTZER fortification.

In the meantime, the Egyptians' harassment of the bridgehead increased in strength and accuracy. Casualties in the 'yard' increased, as did those on the west bank, including the deputy commander of 247th Paratroop Brigade, who was seriously wounded when Katyushas landed on the brigade's advanced HQ on the west bank. Sharon ordered Matt to dispatch a recon force, to stop Egyptian artillery spotters zeroing in on the bridges. Matt's men succeeded in removing all forces threatening the bridges, but paid a heavy price in killed, wounded and missing, as the Egyptians put up a bitter resistance. Bren meanwhile wanted to capitalize on the success of his forces, and ordered Nir's tanks to disengage from the fleeing 25th Tank Brigade, refuel and prepare to cross the Canal. At 21.30 hours, Bren

ordered his forces to leave the refuelling area (those failing to refuel were forced to travel on 'empty stomachs'). He then came up on the division's communications network, and quite excitedly proclaimed, 'Best of luck men, we are crossing into Africa.'

By this time, the 190-yard long pre-constructed bridge, which had been towed forward inch by inch for almost three days, made its way towards the waterline (at the same time a third pontoon bridge was set in place). After the IDF had been on the west bank for one full day and

**Right:** Traffic flows smoothly though hesitantly across the canal on 17 October 1973. The re-emergence of Israeli Air power allowed more tank units to take part in the sweep of Egyptian positions on the west bank of the Suez Canal, rather than remain in the rear to protect the bridgehead. (IDF Archives)

two nights, the Egyptians opened up with a murderous artillery barrage. Tens of thousands of shells were fired from the 17th until the end of the war, and the bridge was subjected to daily air and rocket attack. Egyptian Mi-8 helicopters loaded with napalm were called in for kamikaze missions, attempting to crash into the bridge; even FROG missiles wee fired at it. Unintimidated by this opposition, UGDAT BREN's crossing began. After the third tank crossed, the bridge suffered mechanical breakage which left one tank stranded. The 460th

Armoured Brigade then crossed on Gilowas, although the gap in the bridge was repaired by 01.35 hours on 17 October, and the crossing continued. By 02.35 hours the 460th Armoured Brigade was across and the 217th was ordered immediately to follow. By 05.15 hours, the entire UGDAT BREN had successfully crossed the Canal. Egyptian artillery and aerial pressure was intense. Dozens of tanks were hit and fell into the Canal. The sight of their comrades drowning shocked the tankers, but they continued their crossing. With more than

140 tanks across the Canal, and with each brigade supported by an artillery battalion, UGDAT BREN was ready for the breakout; the 217th Armoured Brigade would break out from the right, Colonel Amir's 460th from the left.

Throughout 18 October UGDAT ARIK was the focus of bitter fighting on both banks of the Canal. On the east bank some major successes were achieved as Colonel Tuvia Raviv's 600th Armoured Brigade, with a force of combat engineers, managed to open up the TIRTUR route. By 11.00 hours, the pre-constructed bridge, towed by Colonel Tuvia Raviv's lead

vehicles, was set in place 1,000 yards north of Bren's pontoon bridges (most of which, after being hit by enemy armour, air, and artillery fire, had sunk). The 600th Armoured Brigade advanced northwards, linking up with Reshef's 14th Armoured Brigade, and seized control of the 'Chinese Farm'. On the west bank, Matt's paratroopers, who held the bridgehead, were exposed to a non-stop Egyptian bombardment. The situation did not allow the Israelis to sit tight on the restricted bridgehead, and at 20.30 hours, Southern Command decided that UGDAT BREN would hold the Genefa Hills, destroying the numerous SAM bases on

**Below:** A Centurion from 217th Armoured Brigade carefully scans the road leading to Suez City. Egyptian commandos were well positioned in the area, and the tank commander's apprehension is quite understandable. (IDF Archives)

the way. UGDAT ARIK would split in two: Brigadier-General Even would take command of the bridgehead (this included 600th Armoured Brigade on the east, and Matt's forces on the west bank), while Sharon would assume command of all forces breaking out in the west, including 14th Armoured Brigade, HATIVAT HAIM and a recon company, and would attack southwards in UGDAT BREN's rear. Morale in the Israeli camp was high. Officer, private soldier, and reservist alike felt that their hour of victory had finally come. Disharmony reigned in the Egyptian camp, as Chief of Staff Shazli, humbled by the deterior-

ating military situation, called for all Egyptian forces to be withdrawn from Sinai. He was relieved of his command and General Abden Ghani Gamasy took over.

Changing the original strategy, Bar-Lev ordered UGDAT KALMAN to push southwards, parallel with but behind UGDAT BREN's push on Suez. The movement therefore became a two-fisted sweep, with UGDOT BREN and KALMAN (on the right flank) heading south, while UGDAT ARIK remained at the bridgehead, and would pushd northwards attempting to capture Isma'iliya. This plan gave IDF forces on the west bank greater strategic depth, and allowed

for the Egyptian Third Army to be totally cut off on the east bank should Suez be isolated and captured.

The breakout on the west bank was scheduled to take place at dusk on 19 October. UGDAT BREN advanced towards the Genefa Hills, destroying seven SAM bases along the way. UGDAT ARIK ran into major Egyptian resistance. It had at its disposal fewer than 100 operational tanks, which were divided into three operational tank brigades (together with covering forces for the two paratroop battalions). The division captured the Fayid airfield, and this was immediately transformed into an IAF re-supply base, with round-the-clock airborne re-supply missions flown by IAF transports. Meanwhile, 600th Brigade, fighting on the east bank, ran into heavy anti-tank forces, and had to hold back from consolidating further ground after suffering heavy losses. The 14th Armoured Brigade (which now included both armour and paratroop elements) crossed the Canal on 19 October, entering into a serious battle with Egyptian forces at the 'Orcha' position. The 14th Armoured Brigade reached the outskirts of Isma'iliya. Sharon urged that an attempt be made to isolate the Second Army as well, and insisted on a wide flanking move to reach the Mediterranean. Bar-Lev insisted that the 'Missouri' position be silenced first, since Egyptian forces there still threatened the bridgehead. The 600th Armoured Brigade managed to capture only a third of 'Missouri', and Sharon's plan was disrupted.

On 19 October, UGDAT KALMAN (attacking ahead of UGDAT BREN) moved on towards MAKTZERA (the IDF code-name for a peak in the Genefa Hills which overlooked the main Cairo-Suez Road). UGDAT KALMAN encountered heavy resistance, and with 460th Armoured Brigade as cover on his right flank, managed eventually to push seventeen miles west of the Canal, destroying large numbers of Egyptian tanks. Meanwhile, UGDAT BREN advanced slowly southwards along 'Test' (a road running south between Isma'iliya and Suez) encountering only light resistance from Kuwaiti, Palestinian Liberation Army, and Egyptian second-line troops, in a succession of military camps near Jebel Um Katib. The 217th Armoured Brigade engaged the Egyptian 4th Armoured Division in a pitched armoured battle south of the ASOR road (a route leading

from Suez to Cairo), and managed to control its northern approaches, cutting off the Third Army from its rear HQ. By 21 October the breakout had been a major IDF success. Although Egptian forces on the east bank fought hard, refusing to surrender any more territory, the IDF had managed to secure itself in force on the west bank, even enjoying a numerical superiority in tanks (420 opposed to the Egyptian 250).

On 22 October, the 17th day of fighting, the Egyptians began to press for a ceasefire. Finally realizing the extent and implications of the IDF presence in the west bank, the Egyptians wished to stop the fighting. Although top IDF commanders knew that the two superpowers would eventually 'will' the ceasefire once the IDF came close to decisive victory, Southern Command still demanded that the IDF further consolidate its positions, and complete the surrounding of the Third Army. The divisional commanders, aware that after the ceasefire a war of attrition would follow, ordered all field commanders (including squad NCOs) to improve their defensive as well as 'bargaining' positions. All forces were ordered to harass the Egyptians whenever possible, attempting to provoke a major battle where further territorial gains could be achieved in the precious time remaining. UGDAT KALMAN tightened the noose around Third Army, while UGDAT ARIK pressed on towards Isma'iliya, and UGDAT BREN proceeded southwards in an attempt to capture Suez. Bar-Lev ordered Bren to attempt to take Suez only if it was not heavily fortified. Should the 'door' to Suez be open, UGDAT BREN was to take the city. Bar-Lev was adamant that Suez should not become the IDF's Stalingrad. The IDF had very little experience of armoured warfare in built-up surroundings, and the prospect of tanks entering a city defended by commandos armed with RPGs frightened Bar-Lev, himself an experienced armour officer.

Meanwhile the threat of commando forces armed with anti-tank weapons continued. During the night of 21/22 October 500th Armoured Brigade's G'DUD SA'ARA (Storm Battalion) had chosen a quiet spot on the west bank of the Canal to refuel, regroup and get some rest. It was dark, and the battalion commander, Lieutenant-Colonel Elyashiv Shimshi, decided it was too risky to continue the advance in such darkness and in unfamiliar territory.

Just before dawn, the battalion was attacked from all sides by a determined Egyptian commando force. Although the commandos were beaten back, and casualties were light, seven tanks were destroyed. The 500th's commander, Colonel Keren, ordered Shimshi to disperse his battalion, and position himself in the open spaces beneath the Genefa Hills, where he would receive further instructions. Two hours later, Keren ordered 'Storm Battalion' (which now constituted one half of the brigade's total strength!) to attack a major Egyptian armour staging-area eight kilometres to the south. Shimshi sent in his battalion's recon company which reported that the Egyptians had abandoned their positions and fled (the recon company later indulged itself, eating large stores of captured Egyptian Ful (fava beans). But as 'Storm Battalion' closed in towards their objective, they spotted a major concentration of enemy armour, artillery and mechanized forces. Shimshi ordered his forces in for the kill. In the ensuing classic tank *v.* tank battle, fought in the open desert spaces, Shimshi calmly led his battalion in a fierce engagement fought at extremely close quarters. The situation was chaotic as tank fought tank five yards apart, and rammed one another when ammunition ran out. But Shimshi's cool and deliberate handling afforded 'Storm Battalion' the upper hand, although greatly outnumbered. Lieutenant-Colonel Shimshi was awarded the OT HAMOFET exemplary service medal for his skill and bravery in the battle.

In mid-afternoon on 22 October, UGDAT BREN once again attacked the ASOR road, this time in a two-brigade offensive. Racing at full speed in a cavalry-style charge, the attack force managed to reach the Little Bitter Lake and the Canal with ease, initiating mass panic among the Egyptian defenders, who fled in their thousands. UGDAT BREN managed to reach 'Kilometre 109' on the main Cairo-Suez road, in effect cutting off the Third Army from mainland Egypt. Bar-Lev, aware that surrounding the Third Army meant its eventual destruction, and a decisive Israeli victory, ordered UGDAT KALMAN to assit BREN in its stranglehold. While UGDAT BREN headed south for the main assault on Suez, UGDAT KALMAN positoned a small tank force on 'Kilometre 101' on the main Cairo-Suez road, protecting BREN's west flank should there be a counter-attack from the direction of Cairo. UGDAT KALMAN headed southwards around Jebel Ataka in the direction of the Gulf of Suez. With only seventeen operational tanks remaining, 401st Armoured Brigade pushed some thirty miles in only eight hours, entering the port of Abadiah by dawn on 23 October. Two Egyptian Navy torpedo-boats in Abadiah harbour attempted to escape to open water, but accurate fire from Colonel Shomron's M-60s destroyed them.

By 23 October, UGDAT BREN had only 180 operational tanks (60 tanks to each brigade). Each brigade had a mechanized infantry company to ward off commando RPG and Sagger teams. Bren ordered no major last-push offen-

**Right:** A SAYERET SHIRION jeep fitted with a 106mm recoilless rifle advances through Isma'iliya, 19 October 1973. Note flak jackets worn by the soldiers, and aerial recognition flag on the jeep's hood. (IDF Archives)

sive, preferring to gain as much territory as possible by small, guerrilla-type operations where casualties would be low. At 05.20 hours the attack on Suez commenced with a two-brigade (217th and 500th) push on the city, together with artillery and air-support. The troops entered the outskirts without difficulty but once into the heart of the city, RPG and light machine-gun fire opened up from all sides, and attempts to extricate themselves from the trap were unsuccessful. Emergency medevac centres dealt with 140 serious casualties in the first three hours of the operation.

In some of the heaviest fighting of the war, most of the troops managed to get out, but KOACH HASDAI and KOACH YOSSI (two tank battalions sent into Suez ahead of the main attacking force) remained deep inside the city limits. Bren, determined not to leave any of his men behind, ordered the division's armour recon company to mount a rescue operation, although he knew that this would be very difficult at night and in unfamiliar surroundings. Under a heavy artillery barrage, Lieutenant-Colonel Hasdai's forces managed to escape from Suez and reached divisional lines

**Right:** Following disengagement talks, IDF forces pull back from the west bank of the Suez Canal. The banner on the M113 reads 'From the war of the Egyptian to the war of the Jews', a dark reference to the heated political environment in Israel after the war. (IGPO)

one mile away at 20.30 hours. Hasdai's efforts were greatly assisted by Major-General Gonen who read an aerial map of the city to the battalion commander over the radio, directing his every move. Safe at brigade HQ, Hasdai immediately attempted to establish communications with Lieutenant-Colonel Yossi Yaffe (who was held up three miles from IDF lines with ninety men, 23 of them seriously wounded). The Centurions were sent to his position under a heavy IDF air and artillery barrage, and although some tanks were destroyed KOACH YOSSI managed to withdraw

from the city. The price for the operations at Suez was high; 80 dead and 120 wounded.

IDF pressure on the Third Army continued without let-up. On 24 October, the IAF mounted concentrated attacks on the Third Army, who without SAM cover and air protection (Egyptian MiGs had also become helpless without the SAM umbrella) were defenceless. The attack destroyed the army's remaining bridging equipment, preventing any Egyptian withdrawal. The Israelis prepared for their final assault on the 45,000 troops of the Third Army, surrounded, hungry, and on the verge of annihilation. Russia responded to this decisive situation by placing her airborne forces on alert, making it clear they would be sent into combat to assist her Arab allies. The United States responded by placing her world-wide forces (including nuclear elements) on their highest state of alert. On 24 October, the superpowers imposed a United Nations Security Council resolution calling for a cease-fire. The war was officially over, with the IDF in control of more than 1,000 square miles of Egyptian territory on the west bank of the Canal.

The battles fought in Sinai and along the west bank of the Suez Canal were the most ferocious in the history of the Arab-Israeli conflict. Egyptian losses were immense: 11,000 dead, 25,000 wounded, and more than 8,000 prisoners of war (although most of these were captured in the closing stages). More than 1,000 Egyptian tanks were destroyed as well as hundreds of artillery pieces and other items of equipment.

IDF losses were staggering as well. A total of 1,450 tankers died in the bloody battles in Sinai, with 3,143 wounded, and 232 prisoners of war. The number of tanks lost on both banks of the Canal was 250.

The 1973 War was the IDF Armoured Corps' true test of survival. On both fronts, Israeli tankers faced incredible military challenges, and suffered extreme losses in men and matériel. In all of Israel's six wars since 1948, no combat arm or branch of service has suffered and sacrificed so much as in 1973. Yet, the tankers of HEYL SHIRION proved their skill, determination and perseverence against superior forces under the most adverse conditions. Israel owes its survival as a nation to the brave men who sport the black beret. It was truely the Armoured Corps' finest hour.

# THE REHABILITATION AND REBUILDING OF HEYL SHIRION

The Yom Kippur War devastated the Armoured Corps far more than any other of the IDF's six combat branches. With so many of its commanding officers dead and wounded, and with so many tanks destroyed and damaged, top IDF commanders wondered whether the corps could recover from the 'October Earth-quake'. Given the precarious situation on the frontiers, HEYL SHIRION was not afforded the opportunity to regroup and quietly rebuild; it was still at war! There was no easy Israeli military victory in 1973. The shock of the surprise attack, with its initial setbacks demoral-ized the IDF, as well as the Israeli nation as a whole. Instead of returning home to jubilant crowds celebrating another sweeping victory, the men of the IDF found themselves still at the front and engaged in a vicious and continuing war of attrition. The tanks lost by Egypt and Syria during the war's eighteen days of fighting had been immediately replaced by their Soviet allies in a massive arms resupply effort. Israel received quite generous emergency arms sup-plies from the United States as well, but with almost all of its combat personnel at the front, HEYL SHIRION's task of absorbing the new tanks and armoured vehicles was an onerous one.

HEYL SHIRION's training doctrine dictated that the high levels of professionalism standard among its soldiers and NCOs be acquired through long training and instruction periods in which indoctrination, combat skills and leadership are achieved over a strictly controlled time-scale. Unfortunately, almost all of the trained tankers (from support personnel to battalion commanders) were stationed at the front; and the necessary time available to train a whole new generation of tank soldiers was unavailable. Major-General Adan (still acting GOC, Armoured Corps) decided that a radical approach was needed if manpower and quality levels were to be increased to an acceptable combat footing. Bren realized that no matter how fervently new tank crews trained, some-

thing vital would still be lacking without the necessary leadership and time to develop their skills. He came up with a revolutionary concept which proved to be astoundingly successful–militarily and psychologically. Bren ordered every tank crew at the front to adopt a crew straight out of basic training. New tankers were rushed to the front after only the briefest of introductions into the Armoured Corps, and were able to train in a genuine combat environ-ment. The veterans at the front were relieved of the menial, though necessary, tasks and overall morale improved. New crews had the oppor-tunity to study technical and operational aspects of their service while actually practising them. In effect, they became seasoned veterans after serving in the IDF for only a few months. By January 1974 Bren was able to boast proudly that not one operational tank in the IDF was without a fully trained crew!

After the 1973 War, the Armoured Corps (like the IDF as a whole) was forced to analyze its tactics and determine future strategies on the modern battlefield. The War had created a political uproar in Israel; a nation used to being initiator and victor now found herself the victim of surprise and unpreparedness. A com-mission headed by the Chief Justice of the Israeli Supreme Court, Dr Shimon Agranat, was formed to determine exactly what had gone wrong in October 1973. The commission's findings, intended to appease a disturbed public, led instead to dramatic political and military resignations (including the resignation of Prime Minister Meir, Defence Minister Dayan, and Chief of Staff Elazar. The GOC, Southern Command, Major-General Gonen was found to have shown poor tactical judge-ment and was sacked). In addition, numerous strategic doctrines in the IDF were found to be obsolete in the missile-age battlefield, and a revolutionary change to IDF thinking and tactics was ordered. Between the 1967 and 1973 Wars, the IDF had been fighting a defen-sive war of attrition which had caused it to lose track of technical and tactical developments. A seriously negligent atmosphere of over-confidence infected much of the thinking of top IDF commanders leading to a lack of initiative in the development of new strategies. The future battlefield, with a marked improvement in anti-tank and anti-aircraft missile capabilities saw the IDF seriously lacking in defensive and offensive responses to these new threats. The 'pure tank' strategy employed by the IDF since the 1967 War was deemed totally ineffectual in a battlefield environment where infantry anti-tank forces posed such devastating obstacles. A combination of all the IDF's combat arms, acting in concert with one another in battle, was desperately needed. SHILUV KOHOT (or 'combined arms') was born. Infantry and paratroop forces were now combined into armoured fighting units, with training and manoeuvres orientated towards the fighting that could be expected on future battlefields.

The task of rebuilding and rehabilitating the Armoured Corps was led by Major-General Moshe 'Musa' Peled, who became the IDF Armoured Corps' ninth commander on 16 April 1974. 'Musa' faced enormous problems. Although the borders were now quiet, and a more relaxed defensive posture was possible, the Armoured Corps still had to be rebuilt from scratch. But the lessons learned in 1973 were heeded, and most tanks and APCs were upgraded in armour protection to minimize crew casualties. The MBT upgrading took many shapes and forms, some quite basic, others ingenious. To increase protection against infantry anti-tank weapons, additional .30 and .50 calibre machine-guns were placed on the tanks. To decrease damage from anti-tank weapons such as the RPG and Sagger, add-on armour plating was introduced to the Centurion and M-60. Known as 'Blazer' reactive armour, these armour plates were meant to explode on impact, severely limiting the penetrative ability of armour-piercing projectiles. Although these additions increased vehicle weight and decreased mobility, it was felt that crew safety was paramount.

Alongside the modification of existing weaponry and vehicles, new items were procured. Modern American MBTs, such as the M-60, and M-60A3 were received in large numbers, as were large supplies of mechanized self-propelled artillery, and infantry anti-tank weapons such as the LAW, and Dragon anti-tank guided weapons. Drawing upon lessons learned in 1973, the IDF also received M113 APCs equipped with TOW anti-tank missiles, and the mechanized M163 Vulcan 20mm anti-aircraft guns. Although these were support vehicles, their weaponry would have an impressive impact in future fighting.

It was still realized, however, that tanks and APCs with maximum armour protection counted for little without qualified and capable manpower. Following the large losses in life and matériel in 1973, very few new conscripts volunteered for the Armoured Corps, and the burden placed on the reservists increased quite unreasonably, and morale declined.

To repair the manpower damage, Peled turned to the IDF's 'womanpower'! Females were drafted into the Armoured Corps and trained to be instructors, first going through full armour proficiency courses themselves. Women soldiers have proved to be more intelligent, disciplined, and well-adjusted to their IDF service, and they met the new challenges with great skill and success. In fact, women instructors motivated the men to achieve their goals faster, because making a bad impression on one's instructor now involved a certain loss of face.

In order to overcome HEYL SHIRION's public-image problem, Peled initiated a programme to increase motivation and opinion of the Corps, from within and without. Junior and senior officers visited high schools throughout Israel, to persuade future conscripts to opt for the black beret and armour badge. 'War stories', illustrating the bravery of the 7th Armoured Brigade, also helped increase interest, respect and, more importantly, volunteers for the Armoured Corps. Peled also boosted morale and performance within the Corps. In 1977, a major study undertaken by the IDF General Staff reinforced Major-General Peled's success rate. Of the conscripts joining the Armoured Corps in August (one of the larger call-up periods in the IDF), more than 85 per cent stated that they had volunteered to serve in HEYL SHIRION, and 97 per cent of conscripts stated that the Armoured Corps was among their three top choices.

At this time the Armoured Corps, together with the Ordnance Corps and Israel Military Industries, was busy working on its most ambitious project to date, a Main Battle Tank (MBT) manufactured in Israel. The search for a modern MBT had begun in 1966 when a few British Chieftain tanks were sent secretly to Israel for testing. The Armoured Corps submitted them to the most gruelling tests and the IDF, quite satisfied with the performance, was ready to order the tank. But following the 1967 Six Day War, Britain as well as other western European nations placed an embargo on arms supplies to Israel, and in 1969 the Chieftains were returned to Britain. The GOC, Armoured Corps at the time, Major-General Yisrael Tal, urged Israeli weapons independence and the ambitious project of producing an indigenous MBT.

The British embargo led government ministers to realize that Israel could not allow her national security to rest with unreliable allies. In August 1970 the government provided General Tal with the necessary funding and support to begin his project, and by April 1971 a wooden mock-up of the intended vehicle was completed and reviewed by senior armour officers. The lessons learned during the 1973 War proved invaluable to further improving the design of the vehicle. Sensitive to loss of life, the MBT was to provide maximum crew survivability, while providing maximum military effectiveness and fire-power. This was achieved by the tank's unique design, with the engine up front, providing a more spacious and secure interior. Although the design hindered the tank's speed, mobility was considered secondary to crew protection and fire power. The gun chosen was the existing L7 105mm gun which had proved so effective against the Soviet-built tanks in the past. In December 1974 the first prototype was completed and ready for field testing. Under extreme secrecy (even by IDF standards) the tank was field tested. Under extreme secrecy (even by IDF standards) the tank was subjected to a series of demanding tests in all geographic and climatic conditions; from the winter mud of the Golan Heights to the deserts in the south. Senior armour officers responsible for overseeing the tests were highly impressed with the tank's performance, and by January 1976, the tank entered full-scale production.

On 14 October 1979, with great pomp and ceremony, the first MERKAVA (Chariot) tank was transferred to IDF service. The first unit to receive the MERKAVA was the famous 7th Armoured Brigade's 77th Battalion, still considered to be HEYL SHIRION's élite. As the first MERKAVA entered official service that day in October, the senior armour officers in attendance, 'Valley of Tears' and 'Chinese Farm' veterans, watched the ceremony in silence as they wondered where, when and against whom the MERKAVA would receive its baptism of fire.

**Right:** Independence Day, 1975. President Ephraim Katzir presents Captain Tzvi 'Tzvika' Greengold with the OT HAGVURA medal for valour. Tzvika refused on several occasions to accept his medal, and was finally ordered to take it by Major-General Moshe 'Musa' Peled. (IGPO)

# 1982
## THE LEBANON WAR

From 1968 until 1978 the IDF conducted numerous military operations against Palestinian targets in Lebanon. These commando raids and retaliatory air strikes were small in scale, and were intended to curb future PLO terrorist acts. Only the IDF's daring commando raid on 10 April 1973, in which the senior command echelon of the notorious Black September Organization were eliminated, attempted in small form to destroy the effectiveness of a particular terrorist group head-

quartered in Lebanon. No matter how hard the IDF persisted in its policy of military retaliation, Palestinian terrorist attacks into Israel from across the Lebanese frontier continued unhindered. In 1974 alone, there were more than fifty reported terrorist incidents and infiltration attempts over the Lebanese border, including the infamous massacres at Kiryat Shmoneh and Ma'alot. By 1975, the Lebanese Civil War had so preoccupied the Palestinian terrorist organizations that their obsession with

**Below:** Dust rises as a MERKAVA fires into a Palestinian Sagger position near Beirut International Airport. Note MERKAVA's unique design, with low silhouette. (IGPO)

the 'liberating' of Palestine became over-shadowed by their desire to become Lebanon's most powerful warlords. The chaotic civil war also led to a deepening Israeli as well as Syrian involvement in Lebanon's internal military and political affairs. By 1978, with Palestinian positions throughout Lebanon consolidated, and an Egyptian-Israeli Peace Treaty signed, the time seemed ripe for a bold and dastardly act of opposition.

On 11 March 1978, a suicide squad of Al-Fatah (the military arm of the PLO) terrorist from bases in southern Lebanon came ashore at Kibbutz Ma'agan Michael. On landing, they killed a female nature photographer, and proceeded towards the main Haifa-Tel Aviv coastal highway where they commandeered a taxi and two buses filled with holiday travellers. Heading south for Tel Aviv, the terrorists fired at passing cars. Alerted of the impending threat, police and border guard anti-terrorist units established a roadblock at the 'Country Club' Junction eleven kilometres north of the city. In the ensuing fire-fight, 37 hostages were killed and dozens more were critically wounded. This was one of the PLO's most audacious attacks ever inside Israel, and the nation was outraged. Clearly something had to be done.

The government had utilized the services of the IDF with great apprehension following the 1973 War. Fearful of investigating committees, and rife with internal misgivings, senior IDF commanders handled military operations with kid gloves. Even during the Ma'alot crisis in May 1974, when Palestinian terrorists held more than ninety children hostage, military action was delayed until the Defence Minister, Chief of Staff and government officials could make their way to the scene, although the GOLANI Brigade's élite reconnaissance unit had been in place for hours. The delay may have indirectly caused the death of 22 of the children in the rescue attempt which followed. After the 'Country Club' massacre, the government decided that a major strike against the PLO in Lebanon was necessary, one which it was hoped would destroy the military infrastructure in southern Lebanon which the PLO had developed during the past eight years.

On 15 March 25,000 men of the IDF crossed the Israeli-Lebanese border. Operation 'Litani' (code-named for the River Litani, in southern Lebanon, which under tacit agreement with the Syrian 'Arab Peace-Keeping

Forces' in Lebanon, the IDF would not cross), was intended to eliminate the terrorist presence in southern Lebanon, strengthen the pro-Israeli local militia commanded by the renegade Lebanese Army Major, Sa'ad Haddad, and inflict as much personnel and matériel damage to the enemy as possible. To achieve these objectives, the invasion force consisted of numerous mechanized and paratroop infantry units, as well as the rebuilt 188th BARAK Brigade, raised from the ashes of 1973. Operation 'Litani' was also the first true test, though on a minor scale, of the IDF's new combined arms strategy. Infantry units advanced in concert with support armour and artillery and vice versa. 'Combined Arms' greatly diminished the threat of guerrilla RPG teams because infantry support teams advanced side by side with tank units. Although there was very little armour fighting (the PLO had only a number of Hungarian-supplied T-34/85s), the week's campaign afforded the Armoured Corps invaluable experience in fighting in mountainous, urban surroundings with a large local populace.

In response to Operation 'Litani', the United Nations dispatched a peace-keeping force (UNIFIL–United Nations Interim Force in Lebanon) to southern Lebanon. Unable and unwilling to curb the activities of the PLO, UNIFIL failed miserably in its attempt to create a peaceful buffer between the PLO and Israeli border. PLO attacks into Israel continued. The IDF began to examine the possibility of evicting the PLO from Israel's nothern border once and for all.

By 1981, the Israeli government had become deeply involved in the internal affairs of Lebanon. Headed by hardline Prime Minister Menachem Begin and Defence Minister 'Arik' Sharon, the government began a long-term covert military and political investment in Lebanon's Maronite Christian Phalangists. This relationship had begun during the Phalangists', or Lebanese Forces', days of military and political isolation against both PLO and Syrian forces during the Lebanese civil war of 1975–6. Seemingly pro-Israel, the Phalangists and their plight struck a sympathetic chord in the hearts of many Israelis Identifying with the plight of the Christian minority in Lebanon, Begin and Sharon believed in an Israeli-Christian alignment in the hostile Muslim Middle East. Many top Intelligence officers in A'MAN warned against such close cooperation with the Christians. They considered them to be ruthless and unreliable, and they feared that the Christians would drag Israel into a tragic Lebanese quagmire.

In 1981, dramatic events were unfolding in Lebanon. Responding to increased harassment of her forces by the Lebanese Forces, the Syrians laid siege to the Maronite city of Zahle. In a show of military support for the Phalangists, the IAF shot down two Syrian Air Force Mi-8 transport helicopters which were reinforcing Syrian positions around the city. The Syrians responded by positioning fourteen SAM-6 batteries in eastern Lebanon's Beka'a Valley. The Israelis vowed to remove the missiles at any cost. During that summer, the PLO stepped-up military pressure on Israel by bombarding northern Israeli settlements with heavy Katusha rocket and artillery fire. Although the United States managed to negotiate a ceasefire, a tense situation existed. Once again A'MAN warned that the Christians were dragging Israel deeper into jeopardy. Many even thought that the attacks against Syrian

forces in Lebanon was a deliberate ploy to inspire Syrian retaliation and an Israeli military response. Nevertheless, war seemed inevitable.

In Israel, training for an invasion of Lebanon began. Drawing upon their own experiences of 1978, as well as those of the Syrian invasion of Lebanon in 1976, the IDF was able to formulate training procedures and routines suitable for a 'Lebanese campaign'. The main revolution in training took place in the Armoured Corps, which was forced to abandon its 'pure tank' deployments and begin training for heavy fighting in built-up areas. The era of tank *vs.* tank warfare was thought obsolete for the IDF, especially for the forthcoming campaign. Instead of battalion- and brigade-sized manoeuvres, tank units were taught to fight along narrow roads in towns and refugee camps, when the main threat would be from the RPG-carrying guerrilla. Training for encounters with Syrian armour was not overlooked, however. The IDF knew that the Syrians (who by 1982 had more than 30,000 'peace-keepers' in Lebanon) were firmly committed politically

and militarily, in Lebanon. The Syrians never recognized Lebanon as an independent entity, but considered it to be part of 'Greater Syria'. It was clear that the Syrians would not relinquish their claim without firing a shot!

In 1981 the IDF was considered to be more powerful and capable than ever before. Under the command of Chief of Staff Lieutenant-General 'Raful' Eitan, it had become a sophisticated fighting force, clearly the most powerful in the Middle East. A new breed of senior officers, with battle experience from the 1967 and 1973 Wars took the reins, while the 'old warhorses' of PAL'MACH fame retired. The junior officers were now seen as the best-trained, highest motivated and most intelligent in IDF history. This was a very different IDF from that which had been caught off-guard in October 1973.

## MIVTZA SHLOM HAGALIL – OPERATION 'PEACE FOR GALILEE'

On 3 June 1982, Shlomoh Argov, Israel's Ambassador to the Court of St. James's, was critically wounded by four Palestinian gunmen as he left a diplomatic reception at London's Dorchester Hotel. The gunmen were all members of the Abu Nidal terrorist faction; a group violently opposed to the 'moderate' PLO, and specializing in the assassination of PLO representatives in Europe. The Israeli government decided to retaliate immediately with massive air-strikes against Beirut, although the PLO there were not directly responsible for the incident in London. The PLO in turn bombarded settlements in Galilee with heavy Katyusha and artillery fire. This was answered by immediate IDF artillery attacks against PLO positions in southern Lebanon. Caught in the cross-fire were the inhabitants of the GALIL (Hebrew for Galilee) who had become hostages of their bomb shelters. The situation soon became intolerable. With large forces still stationed near the Lebanese border since the 1981 crisis with the PLO and the Syrians, Prime Minister Begin convened a cabinet session on the night of 5 June, and it was decided to send the IDF north across the border.

The IDF had three alternative plans for the invasion of Lebanon. First, a repeat of Operation 'Litani'; secondly, Operation 'Little Pines' which called for an IDF push forty kilometre into Lebanon, and lastly, Operation 'Big Pines' which called for IDF forces to occupy large portions of Lebanon, including Beirut and the Syrian-controlled Beka'a Valley, and once and for all defeat the PLO and Syrian domination of Lebanon. A repeat of the 1978 Operation 'Litani' was ruled out for its military futility. 'Little Pines' was confined militarily, but it was considered to be the *safest* politically. Most political and military strategists favoured Operation 'Big Pines' as a long-term solution to the threat at Israel's northern border. 'Big Pines' called for close military cooperation between the IDF and Lebanese Forces, which frightened many IDF planners. They questioned the Phalangists' military worth; noting that conventional combat and military cooperation differed immensely from savage street fighting. 'Big Pines' also risked a major conflict with the Syrians which could easily spread to the Golan Heights and even possibly develop into a superpower conflict. The debate as to which approach was best had still not been resolved at the time of the Argov shooting in London.

For the invasion, IDF planners had divided Lebanon into three main zones of operation. The coastal zone ran from the Israeli border at Rosh Hanikra, north up the Mediterranean coast to include the cities of Tyre, Sidon, Damour and Beirut, as well as all the refugee camps in the surrounding area. The central zone included Marjayoun, due north toward Jezzine, the Arnoun Heights, and through the Shouf Mountains towards the strategic Beirut Damascus Highway. The third, and eventually most critical militarily, was the eastern zone which encompassed the major Syrian zones of control in eastern Lebanon. This area included Hasbaiye, Jebel Baruk, and Lake Karoun. Commanding the advances up the coastal and central zones would be division commanders who were given 'freedom of judgement' by GOC, Northern Command, Major-General Amir Drori, who had been the commander of the GOLANI Brigade during the 1973 War. In the eastern zone, a multi-division command structure was established under Major-General Avigdor 'Yanush' Ben-Gal, who had been Drori's predecessor as GOC, Northern Command. It was thought that a multi-division commander, autonomous of Northern Command, would increase command efficiency and decrease the squabbling so evident during the 'War of the Generals' in Sinai in 1973.

At 11.00 hours on 6 June 1982, the Israel Defence Forces crossed the northern border, invading Lebanon with more than 60,000 troops and 1,200 tanks along a 63-mile wide front.

## INVASION – THE FIRST CAMPAIGN AGAINST THE PALESTINIANS

Brigadier-General Yitzhak Mordechai's UGDAH 91 (91st Division) was responsible for the overall military objectives in the coastal zone. UGDAH 91 consisted of three mechanized infantry brigades (on M113s) together with a crack armoured brigade, the 211th, on loan

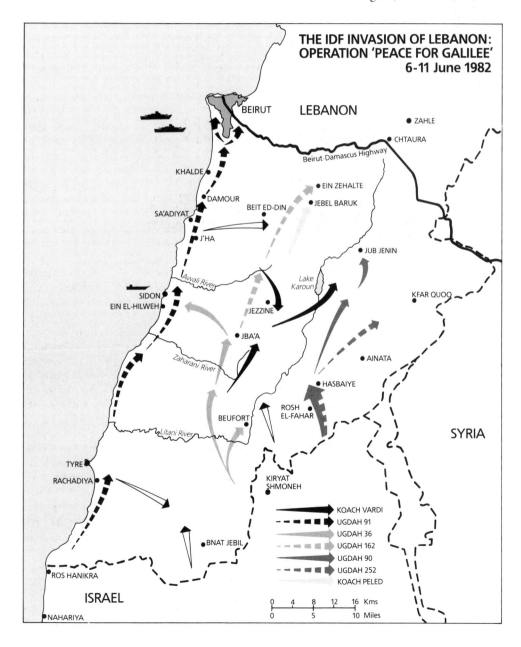

**THE IDF INVASION OF LEBANON: OPERATION 'PEACE FOR GALILEE' 6–11 June 1982**

KOACH VARDI
UGDAH 91
UGDAH 36
UGDAH 162
UGDAH 90
UGDAH 252
KOACH PELED

| 0 | 4 | 8 | 12 | 16 Kms |
| 0 | | 5 | | 10 Miles |

from UGDAH 36. Their mission was to punch a hole through initial PLO and Muslim guerrilla resistance. The 211th Armoured Brigade was commanded by Colonel Eli Geva, a brilliant officer, who at 32 was the youngest brigade commander in IDF history. Already thought of as a probable candidate for the post of Chief of Staff, Geva had seen combat during the 1973 War as a company commander in Lieutenant-Colonel Kahalani's 77th Battalion, and was considered an exceptional field officer, capable of taking and carrying out the most difficult of tactical decisions. The 211th Armoured Brigade was a MAG'ACH (Patton M-60 and M-60A3s) brigade, and included regular conscripts as well as HESDERNIKS (seminary students who combine religious study with military service). These soldiers are among the highest-motivated in the IDF, and are considered fine tankers. At 11.00 hours. Geva's brigade crossed the border at Rosh Hanikra and headed north towards Tyre.

Tyre, a densely populated city in southern Lebanon, sits on a peninsula 22 kilometres from the Israeli border. Surrounding Tyre are six Palestinian refugee camps: Rashadiye, el Baas, Burj Shemali, el-Hanina, Beni Maushou and Shabrika (in order of size). The 211th Armoured Brigade was ordered to by-pass these camps, especially their strategic cross roads which were considered to be hotbeds of determined Palestinian resistance. Geva was to

**Below:** Operation 'Peace for Galilee'. A MERKAVA patrols the streets of the el-Hanina refugee camps near Tyre as 'friendlies' wave him on. The tank commander, clearly apprehensive, searches for Palestinian RPG teams. (IGPO)

advance his brigade as quickly as possible up the coastal road, with UGDAH 91's paratroop and mechanized GOLANI Brigade infantry forces to mop up the rear.

The advance on the narrow coastal road crawled at a snail's pace. The road, twenty metres in width, was surrounded by citrus groves which provided RPG anti-tank teams with perfect cover. One of the support units attached to the 211th Armoured Brigade was a paratroop battalion commanded by Lieutenant-Colonel Uri Grieger. Moving with M113s and jeeps, the battalion was the armour force's vanguard, protecting their sensitive rear flank. While searching through the thick citrus growth surrounding the road, the battalion lost visual contact with the rest of the brigade and went astray. In their attempt to regroup, the battalion ran into a major anti-tank ambush at the el-Baas crossroads near the Shabrika refugee camp. The RPG and small-arms fire encountered was murderous and highly accurate. Two MAG'ACH tanks supporting the paratroopers were hit and immobilized, their add-on 'Blazer' reactive armour saving them from destruction. Other tanks supporting the battalion joined in the fray, as a chaotic cross-fire developed. Tank commanders, exposing themselves to personal danger by standing upright, fired their turret-mounted .50 machine-guns at suspected Palestinian positions. A pitched battle raged ferociously at 'zero range'!

Geva, concerned at the loss of radio communications with Grieger's battalion, peered through his field glasses to the column's rear, only to see smoke billowing from the crossroads. Suspecting that the battalion had taken a wrong turn and was now obviously in trouble, he decided to keep the brigade's advance constant, and send his deputy to extricate the paratroopers. At the crossroads, crews from disabled APCs scurried for cover, as others tried to pull themselves from the burning vehicles to safety. As Geva's deputy brigade commander reached the scene, his tank was hit by concentrated point-blank RPG fire and set ablaze. Managing to escape unhurt together with his crew, he raced towards Grieger's command M113, which also received a direct RPG hit. In the confusion of missile and small-arms fire, Grieger ran in the wrong direction with two of his men and was taken prisoner by Palestinian guerrillas. Their mutilated bodies were discovered in a well days later.

Only concentrated tank fire aimed point-blank at the Palestinian positions managed to end the fire-fight. Geva had requested close air-support, but a debate arose as to its desirability in areas of high civilian concentration. The 211th Armoured Brigade continued its drive northwards. In their push towards Sidon, the brigade encountered a new, unconventional and highly effective anti-tank strategy. A car full of civilians and packed with explosives would approach the lead tank in an armoured column. The civilians, including women and children, would detonate a delayed-action fuze and leave the area in haste. Within seconds, a large explosion would immobilize the lead tank, bottling up the entire column. Palestinian tank-killer and sniper teams would then attack the armour vehicles, caught in the narrow confines of the coastal road. In other instances, Palestinian youths, some as young as 13 and 14, would approach advancing IDF units under cover of innocent groups of civilians searching for shelter. The youths would then fire concealed RPGs and hurl Soviet RKG-3M anti-tank grenades at the vehicles. These children, known as 'RPG Children' had been fighting with Palestinian units for years, and were far more seasoned fighters than their Israeli opponents. Chief of Staff, Lieutenant-General 'Raful' Eitan had given strict and explicit orders that his troops should avoid killing civilians and damaging property unnecessarily. Great care was displayed in the treating of the locals. IDF soldiers administered food, water and clothing to many of the 'new' round of homeless, thrown up by the fighting, even though Palestinian guerrillas hid among the hapless civilians. Although this policy was seen as moral and becoming a 'Jewish' army, it was costly in unnecessary casualties.

By midday, UGDAT 91 had crossed the River Litani and begun their operations to clear the refugee camps around Tyre of armed resistance. By nightfall, 211th Armoured Brigade had reached Sarafend, halfway between Tyre and Sidon. There, they bivouacked for the night, with the tank guns pointed outwards in classic laager fashion. It was the first of many long nights to be spent in Lebanon.

At 09.00 hours on 6 June, Brigadier-General Avigdor Kahalani sat down with his division's brigade, operations, and Intelligence officers and gave them a short pep talk prior to the crossing of the border. It was to be Kahalani's

third war in fifteen years. Rising through the ranks of the élite 7th Armoured Brigade, Kahalani had become the IDF's most celebrated hero of the 1973 War. Armoured Corps training films centred around his career, and his memoirs as 77th Battalion commander in 1973 became a national best-seller overnight. Now with the rank of Brigadier-General, Kahalani was about to lead the future heroes of the Armoured Corps in the invasion of Lebanon. Leading the advance into the central zone, was Kahalani's UGDAH 36, considered the IDF's premier armoured division. Consisting of three armoured brigades and one mechanized infantry brigade, UGDAH 36 was equipped with up-graded and re-armoured Centurions as well as the new MERKVAVA MBT. This was to be the MERKVAVA's baptism of fire, and many top armour officers world-wide were eagerly anticipating the results. At 11.00 hours, UGDAH 36's war began.

Crossing the border into Lebanon at Metulla, UGDAH 36 raced towards Nabatiyah and the Arnoun Heights, in a sweeping move, comprising two main elements. The first, crossed the Litani's Khardali bridge and climbed the Arnoun Heights. The second, crossed the Litani by the Kakalet bridge to attack Beaufort Castle, Nabatiyah, and then meet the other near Jezzine in the Jba'a crossroads. From here UGDAH 36 would swing westwards, and link up with UGDAH 91 on the coast. Although the attack encountered stubborn anti-tank resistance from the PLO's 'Yarmouk' Brigade, the advance went smoothly, the only snag occurring at Beaufort Castle, which was captured by SAYERET GOLANI (the GOLANI Brigade's élite reconnaissance battalion) after a fierce six-hour battle.

In the late evening hours of 6 June, HEYL HAYAM (IDF/Navy) naval commandos landed on the Lebanese coast north of Sidon at the mouth of the River Awali. Here they prepared for the largest amphibious landing in IDF history. Throughout the night of 6/7 June, the small fleet of landing craft ferried men and tanks of Brigadier-General Amos Yaron's (at the time Chief Paratroop and Infantry Officer) UGDAH 96 towards the Lebanese shores. On the beach, north of Sidon, the naval commandos were joined by the 35th Paratroop Brigade's 50th Battalion, which had received their combat assignments at *ad hoc* staff meetings on the Mediterranean. The paratroopers

had suffered from sea sickness on the voyage, and were relieved to be able to fight on dry land'. Their initial task was to cover the main operation, the landing of hundreds of tanks and APCs. The object of the entire operation was to place a large force of armoured and mechanized elements north of Sidon. UGDAH 36 and 96 would attack Sidon and the Palestinian refugee camp at Ein el-Hilweh from the south, backed up by heli-borne paratroopers from UGDAH 91. Colonel Eli Geva and the men of 211th Armoured Brigade would continue the spearhead advance towards Damour.

The amphibious landings had placed Sidon in the dead centre of a pincer movement. Part of UGDAH 91 attacked from the south, Kahalani's division was positioned in the east, and UGDAH 96 in the north. Surrounded, Sidon's Palestinian defenders prepared for the inevitable assault, but a major obstacle was the opening of the main road to Sidon which ran through the Ein el-Hilweh Palestinian refugee camp. UGDAH 91 dispatched KOACH EGOZI (a Centurion Brigade) to join Kahalani's attack on the camp. UGDAH 36, already short of 7th Armoured Brigade (on loan to UGDAH 252, fighting in the eastern zone), encountered fanatical opposition at the camp's gates. Failure to open the Sidon road on time slowed the entire advance up the coast. The 211th Armoured Brigade had to choose between fighting its way through Sidon, outflanking Ein el-Hilweh and opening the road, or by-passing the city and continuing its dash for Damour. A heated debate between Geva and Kahalani resulted in Geva being ordered to by-pass Sidon and push towards Damour. With a large part of his division on loan to other units, Kahalani found himself forced to wait until KOACH EGOZI could reach the division. In a fierce, four-hour fire-fight which pitted tank against guerrilla, Kahalani's armour suffered heavily. The urban surroundings provided perfect cover for RPG teams, which were able to hit the tanks at will. While tank commanders searched the surrounding areas for PLO, sniper teams picked off tank commanders one by one from all points of the compass. The tanks would fire their 105mm guns at a building ahead and infantry and paratroop units would race to clear the building of guerrillas. Each metre of the road to Sidon was hotly disputed and the battle hadn't even begun. UGDAH 36 had yet to enter the Ein el-Hilweh camp.

On 8 June, the third day of the war, the battle for the Rashidiye refugee camp near Tyre was still raging as the siege of Ein el-Hilweh began. Seven years earlier, when intervening in the civil war on the Christians' behalf, it had taken the Syrian Army more than a month to clear Ein el-Hilweh of an armed Palestinian presence. The Syrian Army, not specialists in minimizing civilian casualties, had levelled the camp yet still faced fanatical resistance. Kahalani faced a moral as well as a military dilemma. Ein el-Hilweh had a large civilian population, many being held hostage by the camp's fanatical defenders. The use of massive fire-power would surely limit his own UGDAH's casualties, but result in countless innocents killed and wounded. The large camp consisted of a series of concrete and tin shacks and huts, and buildings reduced to rubble by the 1975 fighting. Each courtyard, alley-way, and side-street provided perfect cover for resistance. In the end he decided to divide the camp area by a grid system. Tanks would cover the mopping-up foot soldiers while the infantry in turn would provide protection for the armour

against anti-tank RPG teams. These force would remain in each grid area until it wa pacified, then move on to the next. The pla worked, and Lebanese and Palestinian nor combatant casualties were kept to an absolute minimum, as opposed to those of the ID whose dead were twice as many as had bee estimated. It was five days before all arme resistance in the camp ceased.

Meanwhile, 211th Armoured Brigade con tinued its push northwards, with UGDAH 9 close behind. At Sa'adiyat, just south c Damour, the brigade came under extremel heavy anti-tank fire. Geva's men managed t extricate themselves from Sagger and RPC cross-fire and overcame the PFLP (Popula Front for the Liberation of Palestine) force o 43 guerrillas. Damour was the PFLP's city Captured in 1976 from the Christians, th PFLP proceeded to massacre thousands of th town's Christian inhabitants. The pan-Arabis Marxist PFLP established bases and interna tional terrorist training facilities in Damour On 9 June, IDF/Navy missile boats shelle Damour from the coast, while F-4E and KFI

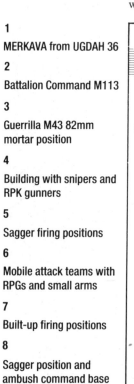

1
MERKAVA from UGDAH 36

2
Battalion Command M113

3
Guerrilla M43 82mm mortar position

4
Building with snipers and RPK gunners

5
Sagger firing positions

6
Mobile attack teams with RPGs and small arms

7
Built-up firing positions

8
Sagger position and ambush command base

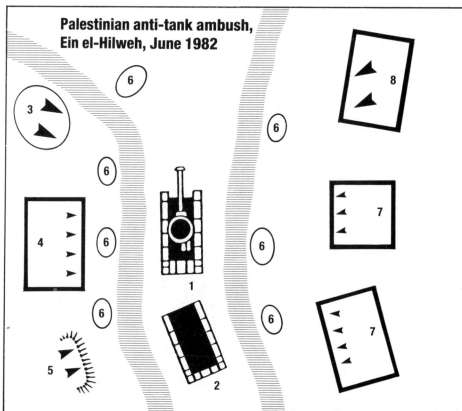

**Palestinian anti-tank ambush, Ein el-Hilweh, June 1982**

C-2 aircraft bombed suspected PFLP positions throughout the city. At 08.55 hours, Geva's brigade attacked the city. Resistance was stiff, as the seasoned PFLP guerrilla fighters made maximum use of the deep caves and ruins from 1976. The 211th Armoured Brigade, seasoned veterans of the Tyre and Sidon battles, managed to overcome the serious efforts of Damour's PFLP defenders. The 211th Armoured Brigade now headed for the true objective of Operation 'Peace for Galilee', Beirut!

Throughout 10 June, mopping-up operations in Tyre, Sidon, Damour and in the camps continued. There were still pockets of substantial resistance throughout the coastal strip, but the push northwards continued and Geva's probing towards the capital brought his units to the outskirts of Beirut. As a result of IAF air attacks in the east, Syrian forces in Beirut joined their Palestinian comrades in battle. The first Syrian-Israeli battle in the coastal area took place in the Beirut suburb of Kfar Sil. Here, commando units of the Syrian 85th and 62nd Infantry Brigades engaged a reconnaissance

battalion from 211th Brigade and stopped them in their tracks.

Kfar Sil saw the first engagement between Syrian and Israeli armour along the coastal front. First-Sergeant Uri Hochshteter, of 211th Armoured Brigade's reconnaissance battalion, having advanced up the entire length of the Lebanese coast under incessant RPG and Sagger fire, had brought his tank out of the front line for urgent repairs. As he approached his vehicle with tools, and snacks for his crew, Uri noticed an unidentified vehicle yards away. Instinctively he slid into his tank, and ordered his gunner to aim at the vehicle. Suddenly, the unidentified tank exploded, hit by another M-60 with a greater vantage-point of the area. The tank turned out to be a Syrian T-62, the recon vehicle of a much larger formation. Grabbing his field glasses, Uri noticed numerous infra-red targets only metres away advancing up Kfar Sil's main street. Allowing the lead T-62 tank to close in, Uri shouted 'ESH' (fire) to his gunner. Uri carefully picked off his targets one by one, as other MAG'ACHIM joined in. A total of eleven T-62s were destroyed in

Below: Excellent view of a modified Centurion undergoing repairs on the coastal road near Damour. Note Blazer reactive armour, and smoke grenade-launchers. The Hebrew word on the mud guard is MAHATZ, or 'force'. The Hebrew letter GIMEL just below indicates '3rd' battalion. (IGPO)

this battle, seven by Uri's M-60 alone, a remarkable feat by a tank undergoing repairs. Although an isolated incident, it was the first major clash between Syrian and Israeli armour along the coast. The Syrians were accomplished fighters, well trained and far superior to their Palestinian comrades whom the IDF had encountered up to now. A cease-fire was declared, and for the time being, the IDF advance along the coast stopped.

The campaigns to 'subdue' the cities along Lebanon's coast had been difficult. IDF men, matériel and tactics had to overcome severe obstacles in its advance towards the Lebanese capital. Palestinian resistance was fanatical in many areas, non-existent in others. IDF casualties were lower than expected mainly as a result of numerous equipment improvements since 1973. All soldiers were issued with flak jackets, and the reactive 'Blazer' armour proved to be an astounding technological success, proving its worth against enemy cannon, missile and RPG fire. The MERKAVA had been bloodied in combat, and although it did not prove to be invincible (as many had indeed thought), it proved to be a superior tank in handling, firepower and crew protection. Yet, the MERKAVA had engaged little armour in the coastal campaign against Palestinian targets. Its true test in armour combat came in the east, once again against the Syrians.

## WAR WITH SYRIA –
## THE BEKA'A VALLEY 1982

It was certain that a major IDF incursion into Lebanon would lead to an eventual confrontation with Syria. The Syrians historically have considered Lebanon as part of 'Greater Syria', and to some degree have always managed to influence Lebanese internal affairs. Syria's role as a permanent fixture in Lebanon's political and military affairs developed as a result of the chaos precipitated by the savage Civil War. It had always been Syria's intention that Lebanon remain factionalized, and deeply divided along religious and political lines. If one particular group seized the initiative politically and militarily, Syrian influence in Lebanon would decline.

When Lebanon did actually split along fa[c]tional lines in April 1975, the Syrians sup[ported the Palestinian and leftist Muslim[s] whose main adversary were the Maroni[te] Christians. By the summer of 1976, howeve[r] the Christian military position had eroded [to] the extent that an imminent Palestinian tak[e] over seemed inevitable. The Syrians respond[ed] by invading Lebanon. Moving through t[he] Beka'a Valley towards the strategic Beiru[t] Damascus Highway, Syrian forces with massi[ve] armour support advanced through the Sho[uf] Mountains towards the Lebanese capital. Pale[s] tinian sappers mined the twisting mounta[in] roads and ambushed the bottle-necked Syria[n] armour from well-entrenched positions in t[he] mountains above. The Syrians suffered hea[vy] losses in men and matériel (many Syrian T-6[2] and T-55/54s were captured by Palestini[an] guerrillas and incorporated into the strug[gle] against the 'Syrian invader'). Only after Syri[an] commando forces had been heli-lifted into t[he] hills was Palestinian resistance quelled. Aft[er] 1976, the Syrians occupied most of Lebano[n] with 30,000 troops under the guise of the Ara[b] Peace-Keeping Force (other Arab nations se[nt] troops as well, but withdrew a short time later[). Eventually the Syrians turned against the Chri[s] tians, once again allying herself with t[he] Palestinian 'struggle'. The Christians in tu[rn] found a willing ally in Israel, as minor cha[r] acters in Lebanon's civil strife found willin[g] backers in the wider regional conflict.

The day of 6 June 1982 was a hectic one f[or] Major-General Avigdor 'Yanush' Ben-Ga[l] Having been summoned back to Israel from t[he] United States, 'Yanush' had not arrived [at] Northern Command HQ until late that Sund[ay] afternoon. As GOC, Northern Command fro[m] 1978 to 1981, 'Yanush' had watched t[he] crumbling military situation in Lebanon atte[n] tively. He had predicted that the IDF wou[ld] eventually become embroiled in a Leban[ese] war, and had utilized his tenure as GO[C] Northern Command to insure proper ID[F] readiness. It was quite symbolic that 'Yanus[h] was chosen as the multi-divisional command[er] for IDF forces invading through easte[rn] Lebanon. Nine years earlier, he had com[ manded 7th Armoured Brigade brilliantly [in] the desperate struggle to hold on to the Gol[an] Heights during the 1973 War. He was ev[en] considered as a possible and likely next ID[F] Chief of Staff. Now, 'Yanush' was responsib[le]

Right: An IAF Hughes-
Defender 500 helicopter
hugs the trees as it heads
towards Syrian T-72
concentrations near Sultan
Yakoub. Both sides made
extensive use of attack
helicopters with highly
impressive results. (IDF
Spokesman)

for 38,000 troops and more than 1,000 tanks, about to engage the Syrian Army in Lebanon. He knew that the campaign against the Syrians could easily spread into Syria as well as to the Golan Heights.

There were five separate divisions, or UGDOT, under his direct command in the eastern campaign. UGDAH 162, under the command of Brigadier-General Menachem Einan, was to follow Brigadier-General Kahalani's UGDAH 36 through the central sector, and continue northwards on the Jezzine Road, by-pass the city, and head for Beit ed-Dein and Ein Zehalta in the Shouf Mountains. UGDAH 162's mission was to outflank Syrian forces in the Beka'a Valley and eventually seize a section of the strategic Beirut-Damascus Highway, cutting off a Palestinian escape route and blocking the only Syrian resupply route to Beirut. To accomplish its task, UGDAH 162 consisted of an artillery battalion, two GOLANI infantry battalions and 188th BARAK Armoured Brigade.

Brigadier-General Emanuel Sakel's UGDAH 252, complemented by two armoured brigades, was assigned the task of cutting off a Syrian retreat to Damascus. Advancing along two main attack routes, UGDAH 252 was top cross the border at the Golan Heights at the foot of Mount Hermon, clear a path through the impassable Wasi Cheba, and head down to-

wards Hasbaiye, Kfair, Rashaye and Kfar Quoq. Brigade-General Giora Lev's UGDAH 90 was to cross the border at Metulla towards Marjayoun, and head for the Syrian military logistics centre at Lake Karoun. An armoured brigade (KOACH SHAHAR) on UGDAH's right flank under the command of Colonel Micki Shahar was to attack along Jub Jenin, eventually linking up with a battalion from UGDAH 252 at Yanta.

Established especially for the campaign in the eastern sector were two major IDF armour forces, KOACH VARDI, and KOACH PELED. KOACH VARDI, commanded by Brigadier-General Danni Vardi, was composed of two armoured brigades (including the 460th under Colonel Hagai Cohen), and was to advance north of Nabatiyah (together with Einan's troops), capture the town of Jezzine, and seize the Syrian military headquarters in Lebanon at Masghara. Brigadier-General Yossi Peled's KOACH PELED, was a mixed armour, infantry, paratroop and helicopter force, coordinated into an élite anti-tank task force consisting of: SAYERET OREV (35th Paratroop Brigade's anti-tank reconaissance battalion), two ad hoc armour reconnaissance battalions and two squadrons of Bell 209 Cobras and Hughes Defender 500 helicopters on immediate call for anti-tank operations. SAYERET OREV's paratroopers, armed with a wide assortment of anti-tank weaponry, from personal weapons including RPGs, LAW and Dragons, to larger weapons such as M113s mounting Tow missiles. No doubt based on Arab units of similar nature in the 1973 War, KOACH PELED's main task was destroy as many enemy tanks as possible in the Beka'a Valley while at the same time preventing armoured reinforcements from reaching the battle by way of Syria. KOACH PELED was to advance past Jezzine following 460th Armoured Brigade and then climb the impassable secondary roads up Masser el-Shouf on the eastern slope of Jebel Baruk. From Jebel Baruk, the entire Beka'a Valley could be clearly seen, as well as controlled.

The Syrian-controlled Beka'a Valley not only constituted a sanctuary for fleeing Palestinian guerrillas, but posed a major threat to the overall success of Operation 'Peace for Galilee'. The Beka'a Valley was Syria's soft underbelly; an IDF push through this vulnerable area could lead directly to Damascus, but in the first few days of the conflict, Syrian and IDF forces were ordered to refrain from engaging one another. There were still fourteen SAM-6, 8 and 9 batteries scattered throughout the Beka'a Valley, limiting IAF ground support for the advancing mechanized and armour units. It was decided, however, to advance as far as possible without provoking a major Syrian response, while political developments dictated developments on the battlefield. At 11.00 hours on 6 June 1982, orderly columns of tanks and APCs crossed the border at Metulla and the Golan Heights. Full-scale war was only days away.

At 08.50 hours on 6 June 1982, IAF Captain Aharon Ahia'az's A-4 Skyhawk fighter-bomber was shot down by a SAM-7 'Strella' during a bombing run over the town of Nabatiyah. 'Yanush's forward command post near Metulla received word that Captain Ahia'az had bailed out safely, but this ominous start worried 'Yanush'. He issued orders to the UGDAH commanders that firepower be scaled down until the pilot was found (in fact, Captain Ahia'az was captured by PLO guerrillas and taken immediately to Beirut). At 11.00 hours, UGDAH 162 assembled to cross the border behind Kahalani's UGDAH 36. Following UGDAH 36's advance as far as Jba'a, Brigadier-General Einan's division advanced almost unhindered, reaching Jezzine's western outskirts by the end of the first day's fighting. Right behind UGDAH

162 was KOACH VARDI's 460th Armoured Brigade, which was given the task of capturing Jezzine before heading eastwards. Also advancing along this route were the anti-tank paratroop and armour units of KOACH PELED. KOACH PELED was to move through Jezzine (once it had been neutralized by 460th Armoured Brigade) and head north-east towards the Jebel Baruk (where the Syrians had a major electronic Intelligence post comparable with the IDF's Mount Hermon installation). Once Jebel Baruk was in IDF hands, KOACH PELED would be in a position to block any Syrian attempts to reinforce their positions throughout Lebanon, and in a perfect position to assist UGDAH 162 should Einan need help in the capture of Ein Zehalta.

Brigadier-General Emanuel Sakel's UGDAH 252 crossed the border near the Mount Hermon foothills, striving for the Syrian lines in the Beka'a Valley. The initial advance was delayed while combat engineers blasted through twenty kilometres of impassable wadis, clearing a path for the armoured, mechanized and self-propelled artillery columns. Armoured units rushed to the villages of Sheb'a in the Mount Hermon foothills, and Shuba in the west, to block any possible advance by Syrian tank forces into the area. The armoured forces (approximately three battalions) advanced through Rashaye el-Fahar in an attempt to capture the guerrilla positions at Hasbaiye. The unit sustained minor damage as enemy fire was poured into its lead company from positions south of the Syrian-controlled Lake Karoun. During these first hours of the war's first day, more than 1,500 Palestinian guerrillas from the PLO's 'Karameh' Brigade as well as 1,000 PFLP-GC (Popular Front for the Liberation of Palestine-General Command) fighters fled to the safety of Syrian lines in the Beka'a. At exactly 17.03 hours, UGDAH 252's reconnaissance battalion moved through Hasbaiye. The force of MERKAVA tanks supported by paratroops encountered stiff anti-tank fire from guerrillas firing RPGs and Sagger missiles in large numbers. Although some MERKAVAS did receive direct missile hits, none was seriously damaged or put out of action. By nightfall, Hasbaiye was declared secure, and the division set up defensive positions on the Ein Kiniya-Hasbaiye-Koukba line.

Early in the morning of Monday, 7 June, BARAK Brigade entered Nabatiyeh. Brigadier-

General Einan feared a fanatical Palestinian defence because there was a large PLO base on the western outskirts of the town. The base was actually a 'terror international' training facility, which hosted terrorists from more than 126 nations. BARAK Brigade commander, Colonel D., had anticipated a heavy fight for the town, and in a stern radio address to his men had urged restraint and caution. Indeed the town was well defended by a battalion of PLO guerrillas with six dug-in ex-Hungarian T-34/85 tanks. Most of the PLO officers fled at the sight of the advancing MERKAVA tanks; and the men, leaderless and bewildered, surrendered after only the briefest of battles. Nabatiyeh fell in two hours.

In the eastern sector, 'Yanush's UGDOT contiued their advance, encountering only minor Palestinian resistance and occasional clashes with Syrian forces. With UGDAH 252 in control of the Druze villages of Hasbaiye and Koukba, the force positioned itself in a defensive line and waited for political events to dictate the next move. Hasbaiye, just fourteen kilometres from the Israeli border, had been controlled by the PLO's 'Karameh' Brigade, and they had done as they liked in the village. As a result, UGDAH 252's commander, Brigadier-General Sakel, issued stern orders that great care and compassion should be shown towards the locals. The IDF had always treated the Lebanese Druze with special sensitivity (a large and loyal Druze population resides in Israel, serving with distinction in the IDF and police security forces) and Brigadier-General Sakel did not want the Hasbaiye residents to consider his forces as 'just another army of occupation'. Many of the Druze elders came out to greet the IDF tankers as liberators, and took them immediately to known PLO arms caches and ambush positions. Mechanized infantry forces remained behind to clear the area of Palestinian guerrillas, while armoured columns continued their advance towards Lake Karoun and the Syrian 1st Armoured Division.

UGDAH 252 continued its advance towards Rashaye in an attempt to outflank the Syrian positions at Ein Ata and Kfair. With only minor military confrontations reported, it was clear that Syrian President Assad was still hoping to avoid a major clash with the Israelis. In fact, Syrian units in the Beka'a were at times ordered to withdraw, allowing IDF recon patrols to pursue fleeing Palestinian guerrillas.

Battalions of heavy self-propelled artillery, advancing behind the armoured spearheads, plotted targets in the Beka'a, most notably the fourteen SAM 8s which now were within IDF artillery range.

On 8 June 460th Armoured Brigade began the battle for Jezzine, and faced the Syrians in the first major battle between the two armies. A crucial and strategic point, a junction near the town, controlled all roads leading to Masghara and the western Beka'a as well as Jebel Baruk and Ein Zehalta. Jezzine was also a strategic dividing line, because IDF control of the town would cut off Syrian forces in Beirut and northern Lebanon from the main power bases in the Beka'a and Syria proper. The road used by UGDAH 162 ended just west of the town, which meant that Einan's forces had to pass through the town. If the IDF could gain control of Jezzine, it would have access to the Beka'a from the west and from the south. Realizing all too well the importance of Jezzine, the Syrians had positioned the 424th Infantry Battalion in the town. As UGDAH 162 had to reach the Beirut-Damascus Highway as quickly as possible, it did not attempt to enter the town that night, although a brief exchange with well-positioned Syrian tanks led to the loss of two Centurions and a M113 battalion casualty recovery vehicle.

An IAF RPV had discovered that the Syrians had reinforced Jezzine with a battalion of tanks and two commando companies on the night of 7 June, but this information never reached Colonel Cohen. He received the order from 'Yanush' to attack Jezzine at 13.30 hours, but he realized he was still unable to deploy his brigade at sufficient strength, as he lacked even the most minimal of artillery support. Nevertheless, 'Yanush' urged him to attack with or without the artillery. As the brigade's tanks reached the centre of the town, Jezzine's serenity was shattered as RPGs and Saggers were fired into the tanks from buildings nearby. The lead company managed to reach the end of town, and destroyed three T-62s deployed as a blocking force. Outside Jezzine, the Syrian commandos attacked the waiting Centurions. Three tanks were destroyed immediately, as RPG and Sagger fire rained down with deadly accuracy.

Tank commanders left their vehicles with GLILON assault rifles in hand to ferret out the commandos in the hills above. The Syrians fought well at Jezzine, and concealed T-62s in excellent defensive positions succeeded in destroying five Centurions in rapid succession. But the 460th's recon battalion sought out the concealed firing position and destroyed Syrian armoured resistance within an hour. By nightfall, Jezzine was in IDF hands, and KOACH VARDI positioned itself in the nearby village of Huna. Later that night, the Syrians moved five new SAM-6 batteries into the Beka'a Valley.

Following the battle for Jezzine, a tragic mishap occurred to the IDF forces, which seemed to underscore a major fault in their tactical deployment. A tank battalion made up of cadets from KOURS K'TZINEI SHIRION (armoured officer's course), deployed on the main road leading to Masghara, accidentally clashed with a tank battalion from KOURS MEFAKDEI TANKIM (tank commander's course) moving in towards Masghara from a southern back road. Mistaking each other for the expected Syrian armour units in the area, both forces opened fire simultaneously, and after the

resulting mêlée, which lasted *two* hours, twelve tankers lay dead, and five tanks were damaged. In times of war, the IDF deploys training units (such as squad and platoon leader's courses) in the field in order to teach unit coherence and give realistic training. Many feel that these cadets are used too soon, and without the framework of the 'mother' brigade and UGDAH.

At nightfall in eastern and central Lebanon on the second day of Operation 'Peace for Galilee', the IDF prepared for major attacks on Masghara and Lake Karoun. KOACH PELED's and SAYERET OREV's paratroopers and covering armoured reconnaissance forces continued their climb up the steep mountain ridges in order to command the Beka'a Valley. Peled's recon paratroopers ambushed Syrian jeeps and staff cars passing along the Beirut-Damascus Highway in an attempt to disrupt lines of communications as well as convince Damascus that a much greater concentration of IDF forces existed in the area.

**Right:** Syrian T-62s destroyed by IDF armour near Sultan Yakoub. Although they lost more than 300 tanks in one week of fighting, the Syrians fought extremely well, earning a new respect from Israeli commanders. (IGPO)

As UGDAH 162 continued its advance towards Ein Zehalta, the Syrians unleashed a new weapon in their bid to halt Einan's advance. At 15.23 hours, tank commanders in one of BARAK Brigade's lead companies noticed unidentified helicopters closing in on their positions. Before definite recognition could be made, the Syrian, French-built Gazelle helicopters fired their accurate HOT missiles, destroying several tanks in minutes. To the horror of BARAK Brigade's tank commanders, the HOT missile's range was beyond that of their turret-mounted machine-guns. Portable anti-aircraft missiles such as the SAM-7 or REDEYE would have solved the problem, but armoured forces were not issued with such weapons. The HOT attack had disabled a lead tank and as a result the road was clogged for hours as IAF aircraft patrolled the skies searching in vain for the attack helicopters.

Meanwhile, Einan found himself under enormous pressure by both Majors-General Drori and Ben-Gal to move on Ein Zehalta immediately. Einan ordered his brigade commanders to speed their advance, but the main road still had to be cleared of the destroyed tanks from the Gazelle attack. BARAK Brigade's ALEPH ('A') Company, supported by a battalion of infantrymen, managed to by-pass the obstacle, and headed towards Ein Zehalta. The Syrians meanwhile were preparing Ein Zehalta's defences; more than two battalions of T-62s and a battalion of commandos patiently awaited the IDF in ambush. Together, the Syrians had almost a full brigade in Ein Zehalta, while UGDAH 162 prepared for the offensive with only a company of tanks! At 22.58 hours on 8 June, the lead tanks of the 'advance' force entered Ein Zehalta. Passing through the village, the few tanks and APCs began their descent into the wadi below. Thus began one of the bloodiest battles of the war. A single Syrian brigade-sized force managed to thwart UGDAH 162's advance twelve kilometres short of UGDAH's objective, the Beirut-Damascus Highway.

Bright moonlight helped the Israeli tanks to negotiate the twisting mountain roads, and most of the armour got down into the wadi. But the Syrian tanks and commandos waiting in ambush realized that the Israelis were trapped and opened fire. The tank commanders had to contend with massive Syrian tank fire from the opposite side of the wadi, while commandos closed in unleashing intensive RPG and Sagger fire. Had the infantry accompanying ALEPH Company been in the lead, the commandos could have been dealt with, but the armour was alone. Two Centurions were damaged and had to be abandoned while the remaining armour pulled back. Panic overtook many of the tankers, and some even began to pray openly on the communications network. The company commander, Captain Moshe Kravitz, realized that the prayers released tension and encouraged others to join in. Without doubt, he was the saviour for many of the men trapped at Ein Zehalta. Going from tank to tank to encourage them (as Brigadier-General Moshe Bar-Kochba had done on the Golan Heights in 1973. During Operation 'Peace for Galilee', Major-General Bar-Kochba was GOC, Armoured Corps), Kravitz also organized rescue parties to collect wounded crews from their damaged vehicles. Captain Kravitz was awarded the OT HA'OZ bravery medal. For two hours the infantry attempted to enter the wadi,

Below: A battalion commander (Hebrew MEFAKED, commander, written on his Type-602 CVC helmet) searches for Syrian Sagger teams in the centre of Kfar Sil, 12 June 1982. (IDF Spokesman)

but the commando opposition blocked them. The Syrians were so well concealed that reports filtered through to brigade HQ that the enemy was invisible.

Upon receiving word of ALEPH Company's situation, Einan called an *ad hoc* staff conference on the road leading to Ein Zehalta. RPG and tank fire from tank and commando forces in well-concealed defensive positions now began to pour into the tank columns on the narrow road. BARAK Brigade, Einan's lead element, began to absorb mounting casualties. Colonel D. ordered his battalion commanders to try to initiate a slow and orderly retreat. But the Syrian commandos had infiltrated in depth and intensive RPG and Sagger fire was levelled against the bottle-necked armour. Tank commanders fired their turret-mounted .50 and FN MAG 7.62mm machine-guns frantically along the side of the road, as a major battle developed. The rare order was given that troops refrain from rescuing crews from damaged tanks and vehicles, as casualties from such actions mounted in alarming numbers. Einan needed his lines straightened and reorganized immediately.

Responding to UGDAH 162's desperate situation, Brigadier-General Peled dispatched his SAYERET OREV battalion towards the highway to attack the Syrian armour and commandos. Racing along the mountain roads on the way to Ein Zehalta, their jeeps fitted with TOWs and FN MAG 7.62mm machine-guns, the recon paratroopers attempted to outflank the tanks of the defending Syrian 68th Tank Brigade. The recon paratroops managed to destroy a substantial number of T-62s with TOWs, but pressure on Einan's forces continued. Massive air-support was needed to extricate BARAK Brigade from Ein Zehalta, but with nineteen SAM sites in the Beka'a, such an operation was quite risky. Defence Minister Sharon, who by now had taken much of the war into his own hands, had the excuse he needed to enlist government approval for destroying the SAM sites, as well as raising the level of hostilities to an extremely sensitive point.

An air attack on the SAM sites would have irrevocable repercussions for the campaign in the east. With the threat of the missiles removed, the brunt of Yanush's forces could move out against Syrian forces in the Beka'a and achieve what had been stopped short at Ein Zehalta. Many Israeli government officials had

opposed an attack on the missile sites, but the débâcle at Ein Zehalta provided necessary justification. One could say that plans to attack the SAM sites had been in a continuous state of discussion in the IAF for nine years, since the initial failure of the IAF to cope with surface to-air missiles. The investment of nine years of training, studying and meticulous planning were about to be realized above the skies of eastern Lebanon. IAF commander, Major General David Ivri, had promised that all the missiles would be wiped out.

At 14.00 hours on 9 June, the mighty HEY HAVIR struck. Israeli-made Remote Piloted Vehicles (RPVs) were launched towards the missile sites, forcing the Syrians to switch on their fire control radars. The frequencies were then analyzed, pinpointed and jammed. As IDF self-propelled artillery batteries began shelling the sites, 96 F-4Es, F-15s, F-16s and KFIR C-2 attacked the SAM sites. Some of the SAM were mobile and as they attempted to flee, a second wave of 92 aircraft swooped in using 'smart bombs' (RPVs with bomb-payload) Without loss of a single aircraft all but two of the nineteen SAM sites were destroyed, and the other two suffered serious damage. The Syrian Air Force responded to the situation, but in three major encounters by 200 aircraft from both sides, in the largest jet dog-fight in aeronautical history, more than 41 Syrian MiG 21s 23s and 25s were blasted out of the sky. In all the Syrians lost 92 aircraft over Lebanon during the first week of fighting. Later that same day, 'Yanush' ordered a three-pronged offensive against the Syrian 1st Armoured Division in the Beka'a Valley. By night, the IAF attacked a column of tanks from 3rd Armoured Division's 47th Brigade, heading towards the Beka'a Valley from Ba'albek in northern Lebanon. The air attack devastated the Syrian tanks and transports, which were left with no air support or missile defences at all. In essence the real war in Lebanon was now under way.

UGDOT 252, 90 and KOACH VARDI moved out against the Syrian 1st Armoured Division in a three-pronged attack into the Beka'a Valley The main thrust, up through the centre of the Beka'a, led through Jub Jenin, protecting both left and right flanks. The right flank, covered by UGDAH 252, headed towards Rashaye. The left flank, to be protected by KOACH PELED, constituted the south-eastern Shouf Mountain area, up to Jebel Baruk, where a battalion of

**Right:** Syrian T-54s and transport vehicles at a position outside Ein Zehalta, 8 June 1982. Note narrow road on which the entire UGDAH 162 advance depended. (Author's Collection)

GOLANI infantrymen captured the strategic Syrian communications and Intelligence installation there. Instead, due to the narrow mountain roads, only lead units were able to engage enemy armour in combat. As a result, a small series of static line battles developed along the entire front. Thursday was a difficult day for Yanush's forces in the Beka'a Valley.

A serious battle developed at a junction on the main road running between Rashaye and Lake Karoun. The Syrians, realizing the military importance of these crossroads, had sabotaged much of the road, as well as having two T-62 battalions in a defensive position to meet the expected IDF advance. At the main junction, a major tank battle developed. It was here that the MERKAVA proved its worth and reputation; many of them, though receiving direct hits, remained operational. The fire-control system proved superior to anything else on the battlefield, and the gunners destroyed numerous T-62s, many on the first shot. It is important to note that not one MERKAVA crewman was fatally wounded in combat, though numerous vehicles were hit. As the IDF armour closed in on the Syrian tank positions, Gazelles once again appeared on the scene. The helicopters managed to damage two MERKAVAS as well as damage a Centurion battalion commander's tank, but their effectiveness was limited due to the appearance of IAF KFIR C-2s called to the scene in desperation! Eventually, the Syrian defensive armour ring was disrupted, as MERKAVA and Centurions charged wildly, breaking their lines. The seizure of the crossroads signalled the collapse of the Syrian 1st Armoured Division's front lines. Although victory seemed close at hand, the IDF still had to break through to the highway.

On 10 June, the Syrian defences at Ein Zehalta were smashed, and UGDAH 162 continued its advance towards the highway. Fighting time and a soon-to-be-imposed cease-fire, Einan raced BARAK Brigade's G'DUD SIYUR to Ein Dara. This town, overlooking the highway, was defended by well-entrenched Syrian commandos and at least three battalions of T-62s. The performance of the Syrian soldiers had surprised and impressed Einan, as well as most IDF commanders and soldiers. They displayed

tenacity, bravery and great skill; especially their tankers and anti-tank commandos. Not willing to risk his best armour forces immediately, Einan decided to call in helicopter gunships to 'test the water'. A flight of Bell-209 Cobras and Hughes 500 Defenders hugging the earth, appeared suddenly above the ravine and attacked the Syrian armour with TOW missiles, putting a number of tanks and BMP vehicles out of action. The helicopter attack also provided a magnificent diversion for Einan to redeploy the BARAK Brigade around Ein Dara, although the town itself was not entered. The Syrians responded by sending Gazelles and a newcomer, a Soviet-built Mi-24 Hind-Ds to attack Einan's armour. The damage this attack achieved was more psychological than physical. The monstrous Mi-24s especially instilled an impressive degree of fear in the hearts of Einan's tankers. The helicopter threat so worried Einan that he ordered extra M163 Vulcan VADs (mainly used in a ground-support role; they cleared Palestinian and Syrian snipers from fortified positions with unimaginable success!) to be attached to each tank battalion.

The attempts to consolidate IDF positions throughout the Beka'a Valley met with stiff and determined Syrian resistance on the night of 10/11 June. KOACH PELED, breaking out on a long, thinly held front, managed to capture the villages of Ana and Zanoub el-Jedida (five kilometres short of the Beirut-Damascus Highway); the northernmost IDF advance of the war. At midnight, however, 'Yanush' ordered Peled to withdraw his forces a few kilometres to more defensible positions before the cease-fire.

Due to to a firm Syrian defence, as well as logistical mishaps, the IDF advance in the eastern sector came to a grinding halt. Attempting to reach and eventually capture Rashaye, UGDAH 90's armour reached a destroyed bridge just short of the town. Forced to wait until combat engineers repaired the bridge, the armour columns bivouacked for the night, planning to continue their advance at dawn. At 02.33 hours, Syrian commandos mounted their most ambitious and successful anti-tank operation of the war. Infiltrating the roadside overlooking UGDAH 90's armour, the commandos deployed in perfect ambush, preparing intricate cross-fire zones, and defensive Sagger rings. The attack shook the Israeli tankers from their sleeping-bags, and they raced for their vehicles. Tank commanders fired their turret-mounted

machine-guns into the groves and stone fences surrounding the road, and the 52mm mortars mounted on the MERKAVA's turret succeeded in breaking up Syrian staging-points. The heavy battle tore apart the summer night's tranquility.

Brigadier-General Lev ordered his armour to advance north immediately, but a chronic petrol shortage had many vehicles without sufficient fuel to advance another kilometre. Attempts were made to get the fuel supply columns to the tanks, but the narrow and winding roads made this operation very difficult. As the battle raged, the road became so clogged with vehicles attempting to advance, that the combat engineers called in to repair the bridge had to literally fight their way to the front. Major-General Ehud Barak (Yanush's deputy, and a daring recon paratroop officer, the Israelis' most decorated soldier and the deputy Chief of Staff today), realizing all too well that many tanks had less than 1 hour's fuel, ordered all tanks to advance, and not wait for the refuelling trucks. But due to the incessant battle and congested roads, the advance didn't proceed until dawn. UGDAH's misfortunes continued when dawn brought an attack of Syrian Gazelles and Mi-24s. M163 Vulcan VADs 'riding shotgun' on the tank battalion shot down two of the Gazelles to the jubilant screaming of the tankers. Managing to overcome the setbacks of the previous night, UGDAH 90's lead armoured brigade managed to reach Yanta, and advance tank battalions of the Syrian 3rd Armoured Division.

Meanwhile, serious operational miscalculations led to the war's largest tank battle. A reserve Patton M-60 brigade, made up of one battalion of HESDERNIKS (conscript Yeshiva students) and two battalions of reservists, made its way towards the hamlet of Sultan Yakoub. Once the village was captured, defensive lines were to be established to hold off an expected counter-attack by the Syrian 3rd Armoured Division. The advance had been achieved in such haste, that commanders from squad level all the way to Brigade HQ had almost no information as to Syrian deployment in the area. Little did they realize that Sultan Yakoub was the staging-area for a Syrian mechanized Brigade. As the Pattons advanced towards Sultan Yakoub's outskirts, Syrian tank commanders looking into the deep valley were puzzled as to the objectives of this small armour force advancing. Nevertheless, orders were given to prepare the T-62s for battle!

Commanding the lead battalion towards Sultan Yakoub was Lieutenant-Colonel (Res) Ira Efroni, an experienced armour officer. Efroni's battalion was considered one of the better reservist units serving in the Beka'a. Morale was high, even though some anti-war sentiments were evident among the men (though by no means at the controversial stages evident among all ranks serving in the coastal zone). The HESDERNIKS, students who settled on the west bank, combined religious zeal, patriotism and combat efficiency; producing fine soldiers. Little did they know the fate which awaited them.

As Efroni's Pattons entered Sultan Yakoub, Syrian commandos fired RPGs and Saggers from buildings nearby. The Saggers, fired from too close a range, missed their intended targets, hitting instead other Syrian firing positions. The battalion responded immediately, with cannon and machine-gun fire in all directions, attempting to coordinate an effective response. By now, however, Efroni realized that his entire battalion had not succeeded in charging through Sultan Yakoub. Some companies were at the entrance to the village, in the valley below, and in the gunsights of the Syrians. Efroni still failed to grasp the extent of the dire situation his battalion were in. As darkness covered Sultan Yakoub, he prepared to hold out until dawn, when a breakout would be organized. Casualties were still moderate, and only a few tanks and APCs had been damaged.

The night of 10/11 June was hellish for the men of Efroni's battalion. On maximum alert for Syrian commandos, the tankers stood by their vehicles pouring 7.62mm and .50 fire into the surrounding areas at irregular intervals to discourage commando advances. Nevertheless, the commandos managed to partially infiltrate the battalion's defensive perimeter and close-range fire-fights erupted. With the morning, Efroni found that they were surrounded, trapped, and five kilometres from the nearest IDF armour units. The valley provided minimal cover for Efroni's armour, but once exposed, T-62s in the ridges above picked off the Pattons one by one. The main immediate threat was from Syrian armour and missiles, but the battalion faced other grave difficulties; it was without its medical officer, and desperately short of ammunition.

Each and every minute, Efroni received word of another tank damaged, another soldier dead or wounded. It is important to note that most of the Pattons continued to operate quite well, even though damaged, a testament to the crews' ingenuity and to the protective value of the 'Blazer' applied armour which allowed Patton and Centurion tanks to sustain direct hits and still function. During the battle, crews from damaged and destroyed vehicles acted as mobile rescue teams, pulling comrades out of burning tanks and APCs, and providing emergency medical assistance. Heroism aside, Efroni realized his battalion was now faced with annihilation. With a mounting toll of damaged vehicles, dead and wounded, as well as limited ammunition, fuel and medical supplies, something had to be done. He called for air support, only to be told that no aircraft were available! Moments later, two MiG-23s strafed Efroni's command post.

Men began to panic as the battle increased in its ferocity, shouting in desperation over the communications network. (In one isolated incident, a tank driver stricken with panic drove his tank away from the battle and, ignoring calls to stop, abandoned his vehicle with the bodies of two fatally wounded comrades aboard. He is still listed as missing in action.) Efroni requested immediate reinforcements from 'Yanush'; who told him that he would have to wait for an hour. Efroni had three options: fight, surrender, or break out! Since all choices amounted to virtual suicide (and the thought of being captured by the Syrians was ghastly), he decided to break out and try to cover the five kilometres to IDF lines at top speed.

Swiftly, Efroni gathered all his operational vehicles, wounded and dead. A massive IDF artillery and aerial bombardment would support the battalion in its dash for safety, the entire Beka'a front having become embroiled by the events at Sultan Yakoub. At 08.45 hours the break-out began. It would take sixteen minutes to reach safety, but all the air and artillery support could not protect the battalion from the RPG, Sagger and other forms of anti-tank fire. Tearing out of their positions with engines screaming, the crews blazed away while reciting the KADESH, the prayer for the dead. At 09.06 hours the battalion reached safety. Four men had died and two tanks were lost. Later that day, helicopters searched the area for the dead and wounded.

**Above:** A MAG'ACH prepares to fire at a suspected Shiite terrorist position in the snowy mountains of the Beka'a Valley. The Hebrew letter GIMEL on the Blazer plate indicates '3rd' Company. (Mike Mairheim – IDF Spokesman)

The cease-fire that had been negotiated through American mediation was to go into effect on 11 June at 12.00 hours, but at 11.00 hours, the Syrian 3rd Armoured Division began to move into Sultan Yakoub; an advance battalion from the 82nd Armoured Brigade equipped with the new Soviet T-72 headed straight for IDF lines. This time it was the IDF's turn to attack. Jeeps mounting TOW missiles were sent in to divide the T-72 force while MERKAVAS, firing from the surrounding hills, picked off the enemy armour at will. The T-72s and T-62s were helpless in the face of this intuitive mobile tank warfare at which the Israeli excel. In the end, more than nine 'invincible' T-72s and thirteen T-62s were destroyed. The battle, an eerie twin of the Israeli débâcle hours before, had given HEYL SHIRION its revenge.

Later that day, the cease-fire took effect; it would hold in place in the Beka'a for the remainder of the war, and until the IDF with-drawal years later. The battles for the Beka'a Valley had been hard fought, and Israeli casualties had been heavy. In the extremely close-quarter and bitterly contested tank battles, the Syrians gave as good as they got, and earned the respect of their opponents. Many acts of heroism were performed by IDF tankers during the campaign in the east, and numerous medals and citations of valour were awarded. The campaign for the Beka'a introduced new weapons to the modern battlefield; the anti-tank helicopter, the T-72 as well as the MERKAVA. The IDF tanker had fought well, under the most difficult military and political circumstances, and against a vastly improved enemy. In one of the great ironies of the war, the 188th BARAK Brigade, which fought so gallantly in 1973 against the Syrians and was devastated, almost met the same fate in Lebanon in 1982. War in Lebanon, and with the Syrians, was not over, however.

There was still Beirut.

## BEIRUT AND BEYOND

'The violence done unto Lebanon will overwhelm you'.
(Habakuk 2:17)

The hard-fought battles for the Beka'a Valley had been seen as a major military victory of the IDF, but Operation 'Peace for Galilee' had had as its main objective, the removal of the Palestinian terrorist infrastructure from Lebanon; a task still not fulfilled at the end of the war's first week of fighting. Many Israeli soldiers began to question their presence in Lebanon; many were heard mumbling, 'What does the Beirut-Damascus Highway have to do with peace for Galilee?' Mounting opposition to the war grew as the exact aims of the IDF invasion became clouded in a growing political controversy. The war in Lebanon was slowly destroying the IDF's legitimate image (both abroad and at home) as a true defence force. For the first time in the 34 years history of the state of Israel, questions were raised as to the moral use of the IDF. Many questioned the validity of the national security argument used as a pretext for attacking Beirut. Nevertheless, the war continued. There were more than 14,000 Palestinian fighters remaining in Beirut; the war could not end until they withdrew or were decisively defeated.

A debate arose among IDF commanders as to what should be done. Beirut was not a solitary position 'holding out' that could be removed by an air-strike. It was a city with well over two million residents, defended by countless thousands of Palestinian and leftist Muslim guerrillas, as well as the Syrian 85th Infantry Brigade. These forces were well equipped and, in the case of the Palestinians, desperately fanatical. If the fighting for Tyre, Sidon and the refugee camps in the south were any indication of Palestinian resistance, Beirut could cost the IDF thousands of casualties. The IDF however expected full Phalangist military cooperation, as the Christians vowed to clear Beirut of the Palestinians 'should the IDF ever reach the city'. IDF military Intelligence had been correct as to the worth of an alliance with the Christians; Phalangist military cooperation never materialized. The IDF was alone in its Lebanon war.

With IDF forces in control of Damour, two possible routes of advance into the city were considered: straight through by means of the coastal road, or by a wide-flanking attack in the Shouf Mountains east of the city. The coastal road was considered to be heavily defended, while the flanking move had several military as well as political advantages. Not wanting to appear as if Beirut were an intended objective, a move through the mountains would surprise the Syrians and Palestinians, cut the Beirut-Damascus Highway quite close to the capital; and close all PLO and Syrian routes of escape. Then intense military pressure would be applied to force a complete withdrawal of all Palestinian and Syrian fighters from West Beirut (the Muslim-controlled half of the city). On 11 June, after a brief cease-fire between Syrian and Israeli forces in Lebanon, the IDF attacked.

The first major battle was for Kfar Sil, which stood in the way of an IDF advance into the Shouf Mountains. Described by Chief of Staff 'Raful' Eitan as the most vicious of the war, the battle for Kfar Sil pitted two battalions of GOLANI infantrymen and a reinforced MERKAVA battalion against two Syrian commando companies, and tank units from the 85th Infantry Brigade. A total of 28 Syrian T-54s defended Kfar Sil, as well as an anti-tank missile defensive line set up by the commandos days earlier. It took six hours of heavy fighting for the armour force to get as far as the town centre. Syrian commandos fired RPGs and Saggers point-blank at the MERKAVA, while GOLANI infantrymen attacked the T-54s with RPGs and 66mm LAWs. The Syrians fought well, realizing only too well that should Kfar Sil fall, virtually nothing stood between the IDF and Beirut. The GOLANI units managed to occupy the Syrian commandos with small fire-fights, allowing the tank forces to clash head-on.

A company of MERKAVAS, commanded by Captain Tuval Gvirtzman, succeeded in destroying sixteen T-54s, thee BMPs, and four transport vehicles within the space of one hour. 'Tuli', as he was known, was highly regarded as one of the brigade's finest officers, known for his leadership; his reputation as a commander deeply committed to his men's well-being was legendary. Many times during the first week of fighting, he would risk his own life to help his men. When an M113s carrying a GOLANI medical team was hit point-blank by RPG fire, 'Tuli' raced to the burning vehicle to rescue the badly burned crew. He succeeded in bringing the GOLANI men to safety at the side of the road, until he was cut down by RPG fire from a commando position nearby. 'Tuli' was posthumously awarded a General Citation of Valour (TZA'L'ASH ALUF) by GOC, Northern Command, Major-General Drori. It took the combined GOLANI and tank force nineteen hours to fight its way through Kfar Sil's main street, one kilometre long. But, battle over, the IDF found itself in control of the southernmost part of Beirut International Airport, and the southern approaches to the city.

Numerous cease-fires stalled continuous IDF attempts to reach the Beirut-Damascus Highway. On 22 June, following major IAF airstrikes against Syrian armour concentrations which resulted in more than 100 tanks and vehicles being destroyed, the Israelis moved. Two Centurion and MERKAVA brigades attacked Syrian positions along the highway from Ba'abda towards Jamhur, Aley, and Bhamdoun. Anti-tank fire was intense, and more than eighteen Centurions and M113s were destroyed that day. BARAK Brigade, attacking from Ein Zehalta, pushed towards

Aley from the east, and trapped large pockets of Syrian forces where it crossed the highway at Bhamdoun. Here the Syrian defence began to crumble, and for the first time in the war the Syrians broke and fled. Ten T-62s were captured intact when their crews surrendered at the sight of *two* Centurion tanks! Suicidal opposition to BARAK Brigade's advance was encountered at Aley, however, which was defended by fanatical Iranian Revolutionary Guards. Many of the BARAK tankers were shocked at the fanaticism displayed by the Iranians, but obliged their wish for 'martyrdom' by pouring massive fire into their positions! Eventually, the IDF pushed all the way down the highway, halting at Chtaura, the last Syrian fortified position between the IDF and Damascus! Syrian losses in the war were heavy. A total of 1,200 soldiers were killed, more than 3,000 were wounded, 296 prisoners were taken, 92 aircraft lost, nineteen SAM batteries, and more than 334 tanks were destroyed.

The fighting along the highway saw the last major armour battles of the war. On 1 August, the IDF laid siege to Beirut. Tanks were used as static artillery pieces firing point-blank at enemy positions, inching their way into the city supporting infantry units. Fighting was fierce,

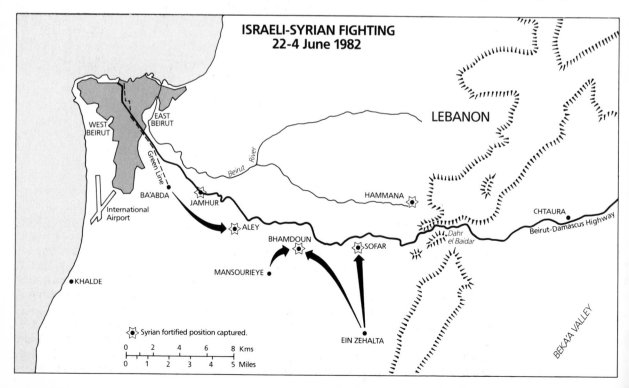

ISRAELI-SYRIAN FIGHTING
22-4 June 1982

LEBANON

WEST BEIRUT

EAST BEIRUT

Green Line

Beirut River

BA'ABDA

International Airport

JAMHUR

ALEY

BHAMDOUN

MANSOURIEYE

KHALDE

HAMMANA

CHTAURA

Beirut-Damascus Highway

Dahr el Baidar

SOFAR

EIN ZEHALTA

BEKA'A VALLEY

Syrian fortified position captured.

0    2    4    6    8 Kms
0  1   2   3   4   5 Miles

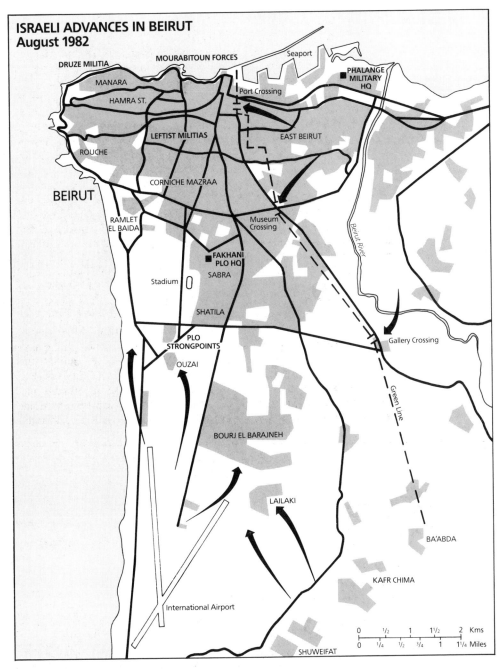

ISRAELI ADVANCES IN BEIRUT
August 1982

DRUZE MILITIA

MOURABITOUN FORCES

Seaport

PHALANGE
MILITARY
HQ

MANARA

Port Crossing

HAMRA ST.

EAST BEIRUT

LEFTIST MILITIAS

ROUCHE

CORNICHE MAZRAA

BEIRUT

RAMLET
EL BAIDA

Museum
Crossing

Beirut River

FAKHANI
PLO HQ

Stadium

SABRA

SHATILA

Gallery Crossing

PLO
STRONGPOINTS

OUZAI

Green Line

BOURJ EL BARAJNEH

LAILAKI

BA'ABDA

KAFR CHIMA

International Airport

0    ½    1    1½    2 Kms
0   ¼   ½   ¾   1   1¼ Miles

SHUWEIFAT

and tanks fighting along Beirut's narrow streets received anti-tank fire from the buildings above to the sewers below. The attack of the city demoralized many in the IDF. In the war's most publicized affair, 211th Armoured Brigade commander, Colonel Eli Geva, resigned his command rather than lead troops into Beirut. Insisting that he would serve in the 211th as a 'tank commander', Geva could not morally lead the brigade when he saw children in his gunsights. He was sacked days later. The Geva affair polarized growing resentment within the IDF towards the affairs transpiring in Lebanon. Before the matter could get out of hand, however, the Palestinians agreed to withdraw; and victory seemed to be at hand. Under the supervision of a Multi-National Force (MNF), 14,398 Palestinian and Syrian

**Right:** A MAG'ACH squad deploys in defensive positions near Ein Dara on the Beirut-Damascus Highway, 22 June 1982. Photograph affords excellent view of the Blazer reactive armour. (IDF Spokesman)

**Right:** Brigadier-Generals Menachem Einan (facing) and Amos Yaron supervise the Syrian withdrawal from Beirut via the Beirut-Damascus Highway. Note Syrian BTR-60 adorned with photographs of President Assad. (IDF Spokesman)

**Right:** Israeli paratroopers supported by a MAG'ACH tank patrol the snows of the Shouf Mountains in search of Shiite terrorists, January 1984. (IDF Spokesman)

fighters left Beirut, the Syrians by the Beirut-Damascus Highway, the Palestinians by sea from 21 to 27 August. Victory and an end to the Lebanon war seemed at hand.

Two weeks later, a Syrian-sponsored Communist group assassinated Christian Phalangist leader and Lebanese President elect, Bashir Gemayel. Seeking revenge, the Phalangists entered the Sabra and Shatila refugee camps, killing more than 800 civilians while looking for arms caches (of which more than 132 were found). To ensure the security of Beirut's Muslim population, the IDF seized control of West Beirut after heavy fighting. The MNF was recalled, and the IDF retreated to the hills. Thus began a costly three-year IDF occupation of Lebanon. A new and more tragic civil war engulfed Lebanon, with the IDF becoming

'captive' participants. The Shiite community, which at first had welcomed the Israelis, now spurred by religious fury from Iran engaged in a bloody guerrilla war against the IDF. Almost 400 Israeli soldiers lost their lives in this bitter struggle against Shiite, Druze, and returning Palestinian guerrillas. Tank units once again bore the brunt, providing the necessary firepower support to infantry patrols. At the time of writing, more than 750 Israeli soldiers have lost their lives in the Lebanon.

The Syrians have once again returned to Beirut; determined to keep their influence alive, but weaker than ever in their ability to keep order. The IDF remains vigilant in her 15-kilometre wide security zone in southern Lebanon, on guard and waiting for the next major war to flare up.

**Right:** A Syrian T-54 leads a convoy of PLA fighters along the Beirut-Damascus Highway towards Syrian lines. (Author's Collection)

**Below:** With the joyous word HABAYTA (home) written on all M113s in an armoured battalion, a NAG'MASH (IDF term for APC) is raised slowly on to a tank transporter for the ride home for which IDF soldiers had waited three years. (IDF Spokesman)

# POSTSCRIPT

The soldiers leaving the desert calm of Metzada after their TEKES HASHBA'A face a difficult three-year future in the Armoured Corps. After they complete Tank School, they will be attached to units throughout Israel. Many will be on guard 24 hours a day on the Golan Heights; others in or too close to Lebanon. Those showing exceptional leadership qualities are sent to tank commander's course, and eventually tank officer's course. In officer's course they learn that the advance rate among officers in the Armoured Corps is the highest in the Israel Defence Forces. To their dismay, however, they learn that this is as a result of the extremely high attrition rate among tank officers in combat. Undaunted they continue their course until once again in a highly emotional ceremony they are commissioned as tank officers. These 19-year-old men become fine officers, creating a unique bond of purpose and achievement with the men and vehicles in their command.

The life of the tank soldier is the hardest of all combat personnel in the IDF. Leaves are few and far between, rest and relaxation a dream. Their daily life is bound by constant training, manoeuvres, and tense alerts. The soldiers of HEYL SHIRION are sometimes taken to the 'Valley of Tears' on an educational outing with a very specific lesson in mind. It is when walking among the tank remains, both Syrian and Israeli, that the young tankers realize their special status within the Israel Defence Forces. For they are far more than average soldiers, they are the ground shield of the nation.

**Left:** Brigadier-General Avigdor Kahalani, 1986. The armour qualification badge and bravery medals worn by Kahalani have come to symbolize the IDF Armoured Corps. (IDF Spokesman)

# APPENDIX: ORDER OF BATTLE, 1973

## NORTHERN COMMAND

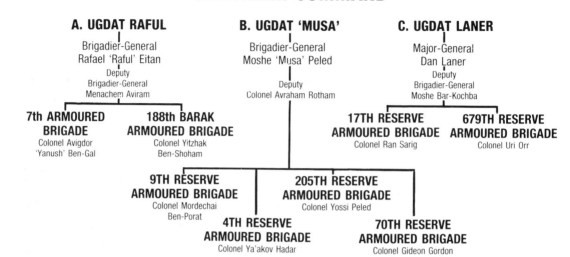

**A. UGDAT RAFUL**
Brigadier-General
Rafael 'Raful' Eitan
Deputy
Brigadier-General
Menachem Aviram

**7th ARMOURED BRIGADE**
Colonel Avigdor
'Yanush' Ben-Gal

**188th BARAK ARMOURED BRIGADE**
Colonel Yitzhak
Ben-Shoham

**B. UGDAT 'MUSA'**
Brigadier-General
Moshe 'Musa' Peled
Deputy
Colonel Avraham Rotham

**C. UGDAT LANER**
Major-General
Dan Laner
Deputy
Brigadier-General
Moshe Bar-Kochba

**17TH RESERVE ARMOURED BRIGADE**
Colonel Ran Sarig

**679TH RESERVE ARMOURED BRIGADE**
Colonel Uri Orr

**9TH RESERVE ARMOURED BRIGADE**
Colonel Mordechai
Ben-Porat

**205TH RESERVE ARMOURED BRIGADE**
Colonel Yossi Peled

**4TH RESERVE ARMOURED BRIGADE**
Colonel Ya'akov Hadar

**70TH RESERVE ARMOURED BRIGADE**
Colonel Gideon Gordon

## SOUTHERN COMMAND

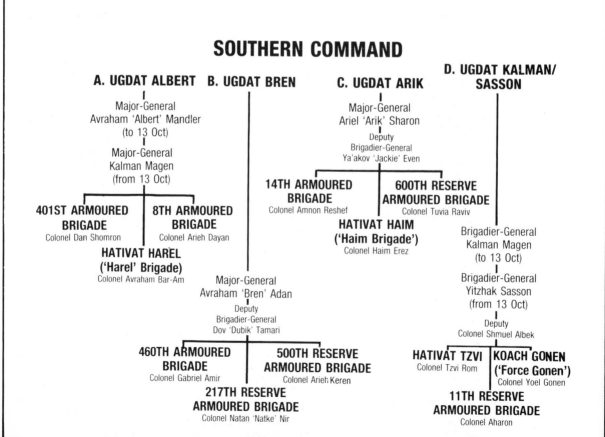

**A. UGDAT ALBERT**
Major-General
Avraham 'Albert' Mandler
(to 13 Oct)
Major-General
Kalman Magen
(from 13 Oct)

**401ST ARMOURED BRIGADE**
Colonel Dan Shomron

**8TH ARMOURED BRIGADE**
Colonel Arieh Dayan

**HATIVAT HAREL
('Harel' Brigade)**
Colonel Avraham Bar-Am

**B. UGDAT BREN**

Major-General
Avraham 'Bren' Adan
Deputy
Brigadier-General
Dov 'Dubik' Tamari

**460TH ARMOURED BRIGADE**
Colonel Gabriel Amir

**500TH RESERVE ARMOURED BRIGADE**
Colonel Arieh Keren

**217TH RESERVE ARMOURED BRIGADE**
Colonel Natan 'Natke' Nir

**C. UGDAT ARIK**
Major-General
Ariel 'Arik' Sharon
Deputy
Brigadier-General
Ya'akov 'Jackie' Even

**14TH ARMOURED BRIGADE**
Colonel Amnon Reshef

**600TH RESERVE ARMOURED BRIGADE**
Colonel Tuvia Raviv

**HATIVAT HAIM
('Haim Brigade')**
Colonel Haim Erez

**D. UGDAT KALMAN/ SASSON**

Brigadier-General
Kalman Magen
(to 13 Oct)
Brigadier-General
Yitzhak Sasson
(from 13 Oct)
Deputy
Colonel Shmuel Albek

**HATIVAT TZVI**
Colonel Tzvi Rom

**KOACH GONEN
('Force Gonen')**
Colonel Yoel Gonen

**11TH RESERVE ARMOURED BRIGADE**
Colonel Aharon

# INDEX